KENT COUNTY
MARYLAND

Marriages

1865-1888

Jerry M. Hynson

HERITAGE BOOKS
2007

HERITAGE BOOKS

AN IMPRINT OF HERITAGE BOOKS, INC.

Books, Cds, and more—Worldwide

For our listing of thousands of titles see our website
at
www.heritagebooks.com

Published 2007 by
HERITAGE BOOKS, INC.
Publishing Division
65 East Main Street
Westminster, Maryland 21157-5026

International Standard Book Number: 978-0-7884-3576-0

Contents

Introduction

The exploration of African American Family Histories or Genealogies continues to grow at an exponential rate. This growth has led to an increased demand for research aids to be used by those who cannot travel to local courthouses or record depositories for marriage records. This research reference is an attempt to make such records more readily available.

The research was hindered by the usual problems of the Family Historian, including poor film quality, incomplete records, unusual spelling of names, and illogical entries of dates. In reference to the latter it was found that in some cases the 'date of the recording of the marriage' preceded the' date of the marriage.' In such cases the dates of record were not changed in this publication. While it is our opinion that this error resulted from a transcription error, we do not find sufficient evidence to warrant the changes suggested by the apparent error.

In cases of unusual name spelling, the original spelling is followed by '/ suggested name'. In some cases the misspelling was not the subject of correction. This decision was based on the author's personal knowledge of the parties involved. For example, 'Hynson' is sometimes rendered 'Hinson', or 'Henson'. Since there are families utilizing one or more of these spellings, the records were left intact with no suggested correction.

In addition, we have utilized the records of marriages from the Kent County, Maryland Courthouse as the basis for this work. We have not included the records of marriage licenses issued, since the issuance of a license does not indicate the fact of an actual marriage.

This record of marriages has been derived from the Maryland State Archives microfilm # MSA M 218. The microfilm can be viewed at The Maryland State Archives, Annapolis, Maryland. The reader is urged to consult this film in person before drawing a positive conclusion about a given marriage.

The records are arranged alphabetically by the groom's surname. The records are presented in the following order: Name of the Groom, with his age, marital status, and occupation, location other than Kent County; Name of Bride with her age, marital status, and occupation, location other than Kent; marriage date; marriage recorded date.

The index is to the bride's maiden name only.

v

----; Jones, Augusta; 18 February 1868

----; Jones, Hester, 23, single, cook; 6 June 1873

----; Tillison, Mary, 22, widow; 5 December 1882

Adams, Charles, 20, single, farmhand; Burgen, Louisa, 16, single, not employed; 16 December 1878; 28 December 1878

Allen, Josiah, 27, single, Hostler; Trusty, Hannah, 16, single, cook; 14 April 1885; 20 April 1885

Anderson, Benjamin, 20, single, laborer; Scott, Sarah, 20, single, servant; 13 August 1868; 14 November 1868

Anderson, Chester, 58, widower, laborer; Gunn/Dunn, Lucinda; 51, widow; 1867; 14 June 1867

Anderson, George T., 25, single, farmer; Brown, Ellen, 27, single; 16 Oct, 1885; 30 August 1885

Anderson, George, 24, single, laborer; Plater, Lizzie, 20, single, cook; 15 January 1869; 26 July 1869

Anderson, John W, 28, laborer, single; Wright, Emma A, 18, single, not employed; 4 June 1873

Anderson, John W., 30, widower, carter; Anderson, Renora, 26, cook; 8 September 1877; 22 April 1880

Anderson, Joseph, 24, farmhand, single; Neal, Louisa, 21, single, cook; January 1871; 16 June 1871

Anderson, Joseph, 27, widower, farmhand; Jackson, Tiny, 28, servant; 3 February 1875; 20 March 1875

Anderson, Joshua, 23, farmer, single; Henry, Sarah Maria, 18, servant, single; 9 April 1874; 25 May 1874

Anderson, Louis, 21, farmhand, single; Jones, Mary A., 19, single, cook; 2 Nov. 1882; 5 December 1882

Anderson, Noble, 56, widower, laborer; Finch, Elizabeth, 40, widow, cook; 12 May 1881; 3 November 1881

Anderson, Perry Wright, 17, farmer, single; Raisin, Rachel S., 19, servant; 24 September 1869; 7 October 1870

Anderson. Perry, 50, single, farmhand; Ward, Julia, 36, cook, single; 23 December 1877; 26 January 1878

Ashley, Thomas; 35, widower, laborer; Hemsley, Delinda, 30, single, servant; 1867; 14 June 1867

Bailey, John C., 37, widower, waiter; Granger, Hester, 27, widow; 17 December 1882; 16 March 1883

Baker, Issac, 25, single, farmhand; Reese, Emma, 22 single, cook; 21 September 1885; 25 September 1885

Banks, Alfred, 21, single, laborer; Turner, Emma, 22, single, not employed; 14 May 1880; 18 May 1880

Banks, Archer, 25, single, laborer; Anderson, Mary, 24, single, cook; 29 December 1869; 16 June 1870

Banks, George, 22, single, farmhand; Mathias, Eliza, 19, single; 15 June 1886; 17 June 1886

Banks, Hambleton, 21, gentleman; Anderson, Mary, 19, single, lady; 25 December 1874; 1 August 1874

Banks, Henry, 23, single, farmhand, Cecil Co; Black, Maria, 22, single, servant, Cecil Co; illegible; 26 June 1869

Banks, John, 20, laborer, single; Toomy, Easter J., 18, servant, single; 15 August 1869; 5 January 1870

Banner, Daniel, 22, single, farmhand; Kennard, Jane, 20, single, house girl; 29 December 1880; 9 February 1881

Barlow, John H. D. William, 20, single, farmhand; Butler, Henrietta Brown, 15, single, cook; 24 Aug. 1877; 22 April 1880

Barrett, Charles Henry, 30, widower, farm hand; Whittingham, Nancy, 35, widow, servant; 23 August 1875; 14 December 1875

Barrett, Charles Henry, 30, widower, farmhand; Whittingham, Nancy, 35, widow, servant; 23 August 1875; 14 December 1875

Barrett, John, 33, laborer, single; Jacobs, Annie, 18, single, cook; 20 July 1881; 9 August 1881

Barrett, Levi R., 23, single, laborer; Blake, Emma C., 21, single, servant; 16 January 1873; 1 March 1873

Barroll, Edward, single, 28, laborer; Hornsby, Jane, 30, cook, single; 28 December 1876; 21 August 1877

Barroll, George, 30, farmhand; Cotton, Caroline, 20, single; 30 December 1874; 31 December 1874

Barroll, George, 30, single, farm hand; Cotton, Caroline, 20, single, servant; 30 December 1874; 31 December 1874

Barroll, Pere, 25, single, farm hand; Thompson, Ellen, 20, single, servant; 29 March 1875; 30 March 1875

Barroll, Pere, 25, single, farmhand; Thompson, Henrietta, 20, single, servant; 29 March 1875; 30 March 1875

Bastow, Asbury, 25 single, farmhand. This appears to be lined out; Wilmer, Ella Jane, 23, single, cook; 16 Oct. 1879; 27 October 1879

Bateman, William, 25, widower, farmhand; Keys, Lizzie, 25, widow, cook; 25 May 1885; 26 May 1885

Bateman, William, 35, single, laborer; Asbury, Harriet, 38, widow, not employed; 17 May 1880; 19 May 1880

Bateman, William, 40, widower, farmhand; Keys, Lizzie, 25, widow, cook; 25 May 1885; 26 May 1885

Bean, Somerset, 24, farm hand, single; Butler, Sarah, 20, single; 5 April 1874; 11 August 1876

Bean, Somerset, 24, farmhand; Butler, Sarah, 20, single; 5 April 1874; 11 August 1874

Beck/LeBeck, John/John L., 21, single, laborer; Newman, Anna M., 19, single, house maid; 4 June 1868; 10 August 1868

Bell, Mitchell, 45, widower, laborer; Ashley, Susan, 47, widow, cook; 16 January 1884; 31 March 1884

Benson, Charles, 24, single, farmhand; Clayton, Ann Maria, 16, single, house girl; 22 April 1884; 7 May 1884

Benson, Stephen, 23, single, laborer; Steward, Lizzie, 19, single, cook; 5 June 1872; 7 June 1872

Bentley, Adam, 42, single, laborer; Banks, Rachel, 18, single, cook; 18 December 18713; 24 July 1875

Benton, John F, 25, laborer, single; Brown, Harriet, 20, servant, single; 19 August 1869; 22 December 1869

Benton, John, 47, widower, laborer; Simmons, Ellen, 45, widow; 24 May 1868; 25 June 1868

Berman, George, 60, farmer; Crage/Craig, Nancy, 50, single, servant; 2 December 1876; 21 July 1877

Berry, Alexander; Berry, Susan Ann; 12 July 1867; 25 June 1868

Berry, George, 22, single, laborer; Collins, Rosanna, 20, single, servant; 28 Jan. 1869; 7 April 1869

Berryman, Charles, 43, single, widower; Madison, Frances, 35, single, cook; 6 October 1882; 17 October 1882

Bessicks, Robert, 21, oysterman; Ringgold, Hannah E., 16, single, cook; 15 October 1884; 17 December 1884

Bessicks, Robert, 21, single, oysterman; Ringgold, Hannah, 16, single, cook; 15 October 1884; 17 December 1884

Black, Joseph, 25, single, farmhand; Johnson, Maria, 28, single, cook; 28 December 1876; 3 February 1877

Black, Levi, 23, single, laborer; Jones, A. M. A., 16, single, cook; 10 December 1885; 15 January 1886

Black, Samuel, 22, single, farmhand; Moore, Ella, 23, single, cook; 21 May 1885; 9 June 1885

Black, Samuel, 22, single, farmhand; Moore, Ella, 23, single, cook; 21 May 1885; 9 August 1885

Black, Southren, 25, single, laborer; Tilghman, Annie, 30, single, servant; 29 Oct. 1868; 24 September 1869

Blackiston, James, 24, single, farmhand; Cotton, Julia, 20, single, house servant; 16 June 1881; 3 September 1881

Blackiston, Washington, 24, single, farmhand, born Essex Co., Va; Butler, Millicent, 22, housework, single; 30 December 1880; 31 December 1880

Blackistone, John R., 23, single, laborer; Brown, Sarah M., 16, single, servant; 22 October 1868; 16 January 1869

Blackson, Philip Webster, 23, single, farmhand; Turner, Mary Isabella, 15, single, cook; 13 October 1876

Blackwell, Thomas, 30, single, farmer; Graves, Martha, 20, single, cook; Jan. 1869; 16 April 1869

Blair, James, 25, single, farmhand; Green, Ella, 19, single, cook; 2 July 1885; 1 February 1887

Blake James H., 21 single, farmhand; Hynson, Harriet A., 19, single; 25 December 1882; 29 December 1882

Blake, Charles H., 25, single, barber; Butcher, Fanny, 24, single, servant; 27 May 1879; 22 April 1880

Blake, E. Henry, 40, single, farmer; Boyer, M. Rebecca; 1866; 9 August 1867

Blake, Ebenezer, 24, single, farmhand; Cammile, Martha A., 18, single, house girl; 15 December 1881; 4 April 1882

Blake, Ezekiel, 21, single, laborer; Reynolds, Henrietta, 20, single; 30 December 1873; 12 December 1873

Blake, George Thomas, 28, single, laborer; Hackett, Lizzie, 20, single, cook; 15 November 1883; 4 April 184

Blake, John F., 23, single, farmhand; Butler, Lena, 19, single, cook; 6 April 1885; 20 April 1885

Blake, John F., 23, single, farmhand; Butler, Lena, 19, single, cook; 6 April 1885; 20 April 1885

Blake, Simon, 45, single, farm hand; Ringgold, Henrietta, 36, single, cook; 1 Aug. 1879; 8 August 1879

Boardley, George, 28, single, laborer; Thompson, Alice, 26, single, cook; 4 March 1884; 4 March 1884

Booker, William, 23, single, laborer; Hurtt, Eliza, 20, house servant; 18 April 1869; 20 April 1869

Bordley, Charles, 27, single, farmhand; Spencer, Lucy, 24, single, cook; 16 Oct. 1879; 27 October 1879

Bordley, Emory, 35, single, laborer; Worrell, Susan, 30, single, cook; 21 September 1869; 6 January 1870

Bordley, Richard J., 33, single, farmhand; Cooper, Mary L., 22, single; 13 October 1885; 23 December 1885

Bordley, Simon, 24, single, hostler; Gould, Charlotte L., 27, single, cook; 22 September 1881; 10 November 1881

Bordley, William, 26, single, laborer, Queen Anne's Co; Green, Jane, 31, widow, cook, Queen Anne's Co; 27 December 1874; 24 July 1874

Bordley, William, 26, single, laborer, resides in Queen Anne; Green, Jane, 30, widow, cook, resides in Queen Ann; 27 December 1874; 24 July 1875

Bosley, John, 22, single, farm hand; Jones, Harriett Rebecca, 18, single, servant; 13 December 1876; 10 April 1876

Bosley, John, 22, single, farmhand; Jones, Harriett Rebecca, 18, single, servant; 13 Dec. 1876; 10 April 1876

Boughton, Isaiah, single, clergyman; Eves, Martha, single; 22 December 1868; 2 January 1869

Boulden, Walter, 40, single, laborer; Bayman, Mary, 25, single; 20 Mar. 1869; 26 June 1869

Bowen, Thomas, 21, single, laborer; Turner, Georgianna, 20, single, cook; 28 December 1872; 25 June 1873

Bowen, William, 28, single, laborer; Graves, Josephine, 20, single, servant; 20 November 1872; 3 May 1873

Bowers, Alexander, 25, single, farmhand; Blackiston, Cora, 18, waitress; 26 April 1876; 2 October 1876

Bowers, Alexander, 26, single, farmer; Blackistone, Cora, 18, single, waitress; 26 April 1876; 2 October 1876

Bowers, L. H. T., 21, laborer; Wilson, Editha, 16, single, house cook; 28 Dec. 1878; 26 January 1878

Bowser, Alexander, 35, widower, farmer; Sudler, Julia, 25, single, cook; 18 January 1883; 9 May 1883

Bowser, Joseph, 22, single, farmhand; Butler, Harriet, 18, single, house girl; 19 December 1882; 15 January 1883

Bowser, Philip, 46, widower, farmhand; Blake, Martha, 40 single, cook; 8 January 1882; 18 February 1882

Bowsers, Alex, 21, single, laborer; Flamer, Ellen, 23, single, cook; 20 November 1872; 3 May 1873

Boyce, Robert, 31, widower, blacksmith; Gould, Susan, 21, single; 2 December 1864; 20 June 1868

Boyer, August, 26, single; Hall, Mary J., 24, single; 5 November 1885; 9 November 1885

Boyer, David H., 28, single, farmer; Ashley, Mary I., 26, Queen Anne's Co., house maid; 10 April 1884; 16 April 1884

Boyer, Isaac, single, laborer; Brown, Geraldine, 19, single, cook; 22 December 1870; 27 March 1871

Boyer, Richard, 25, single, laborer; Frisby, Julia, 19, servant; 27 September 1866; 7 February 1867

Boyer, Richard, 42, widower, gardener; Murray, Lydia, 22, single, cook; 4 December 1884; 21 Febru7ary 1885

Boyer, Richard, 42, widower, gardener; Murray, Lydia, 22, single, cook; 4 December 1884; 21 February 1885

Boyer, Wesley, 31, single, laborer; Smith, Gracie, 25, single, cook; 15 June 1880; 23 June 1880

Boyer, William W., 25, single, laborer; Jones, Elizabeth, 21, single, cook; 20 November 1884; 25 November 1884

Boyer, William W., 25, single, laborer; Jones, Elizabeth, 21, single, cook; 20 November 1884; 25 November 1884

Bracher, Samuel, single, farmer; Riley, Harriet A., single, cook; 5 December 1872; 6 June 1873

Bradshaw John _, single, laborer; Chambers, Mary C., single; 30 Dec. 1867; 9 April 1868

Bradshaw, George W., 30, single, farmhand; Wilmer, Alice A., 19, single, dressmaker; 12 December 1873; 6 May 1874

Bradshaw, John, 22, single, laborer; Forman, Sarah E., 22, single, cook; 18 May 1873; 25 June 1873

Brandenburg, Abel, 23, single, laborer; Nichols, Ann, 27, single, servant; 6 Nov. 1867; 1 April 1869

Brice, Thomas A., 25, single, farmhand; Grinett, Fannie L., 20, single, cook; 11 October 1883; 18 October 1883

Brickus, William Henry, 27, single, laborer, b. Springfield City; Tempy, Ann Veal, 26, single, widow, b. Cecil Co, s; 3 Jan. 1878; 1 September 1878

Brinkley, William Henry, 24, single, farmhand; Brooks, Annie, 19, single, cook; 19 June 1884; 26 June 1884

Brinkley, William Henry, 24, single, farmhand; Brooks, Annie, 19, single, cook; 19 June 1884; 26 June 1884

Briscoe, Ezekiel, 24, single; Scott, Hester, 17, single; 10 Dec. 1869; 26 July 1869

Broadway, John W., 24, single, laborer; Rees, Annie Ell, 22, single, cook; 27 Dec. 1879; 22 April 1880

Broadway, Joseph, 35, laborer; Wright, Emily, 27, servant; 22 April 1869; 15 June 1869

Brookings, Phillip, 29, laborer, single; Brown, Willie, 15, single, servant; not legible; 5 June 1867

Brookins, Charles, 23, single, laborer; Blake, Julia A., 21, servant, single; 18 July 1868; 16 January 1869

Brooks, Alexander, 25, single, farmhand; Thomas, Lizzie, 18, single, cook; 9 December 1880; 9 February 1881

Brooks, Charles H., 27, single, farmhand; Sanders, Anna R., 20, single, cook; 28 July 1885; 4 August 1885

Brooks, Charles H., 27, single, farmhand; Sanders, Annie R., 20, single, cook; 28 July 1885; 4 August 1885

Brooks, Daniel, 22, single, ostler; Johnson, Mary A., 21, single, cook; 1884; 15 November 1884

Brooks, Daniel, 22, single, ostler; Johnson, Mary A., 21, single, cook; January 1884; 15 November 1884

Brooks, George Washington, 254, single, laborer; Wright, Lizzie, 18, single, cook; 17 Oct. 1879; 22 April 1880

Brooks, James A., 21, single, farmhand; Saunders, Julia, 18, single, cook; 26 Oct. 1880; 23 November 1880

Brooks, John H., single, laborer; Wright, Mary F., single, cook; 7 March 1872; 7 August 1872

Brooks, Richard, 20, single, laborer; Ringgold, Minty, 23, single; 5 March 1868; 10 August 1868

Brown Isaiah, 25, single, farmer; Anderson, Jane, 20, single, servant; 24 October 1876; 24 October 1876

Brown, Alex., 21, single, laborer; Caulk, Martha J., 19, single, cook; 21 December 1870; 27 March 1871

Brown, Alexander, 26, single, farmhand; Fisher, Georganna, 25, single, servant; 30 August 1877; 12 September 1877

Brown, Alexander, 30, single, laborer; Ford, Lillie, 26, single, cook; 30 December 1885; 16 March 1886

Brown, Benjamin W, 25, single, farmhand; Brown, Hannah, 22, single, cook; 8 June 1885; 26 June 1885

Brown, Charles, 22, single, farmhand; Bordley, Georgianna, 22, single, cook; 29 December 1881; 4 April 1882

Brown, Daniel, 35, single, farm hand; Blake, Mary, 45, widow, cook; 24 April 1879; 25 April 1879

Brown, Edwin, 26, single, laborer; Brown, Lucy, 24, single, cook; 18 March 1880; 2 December 1882

Brown, Emory, 72, widower, farmhand; Wallis, Rachel, 45, single, cook; 29 September 1882; 1 October 1882

Brown, Ezekiel, 25, laborer, single; Boyer, Josephine, 20, servant, single; 15 June 1869; 22 December 1869

Brown, G. W., 23, single, farm hand; Berryman, Anna, 21, single, servant; 1 Dec/ 1870; 16 January 1878

Brown, George H., 38, laborer; Lee, Prissy, 38, servant; 18 April 1866; 7 October 1866

Brown, George W, 23, single, farmhand; Frisby, Margaret, 20, single, cook; 17 December 1885; 18 December 1885

Brown, George W., 24, single, school teacher; Brown, Mary C., 20, single, lady; 6 April, 1885; 10 June 1885

Brown, George, 21, single, farmhand; Starling, Caroline, 16, single, servant; Jan. 1878; 1 July 1878

Brown, George, 21, single, laborer, Queen Anne's Co; Bennett, Annie Isabella, 18, single, cook; 6 January 1886; 15 January 1886

Brown, George, 25, single, Laborer; Leatherberry, Caroline, 25, widow, servant; 17 December 1871; 1 August 1867

Brown, George, 25, single, laborer; Leatherberry, Caroline, 25, widow, servant; 17 December 1874; 1 August 1874

Brown, Harrison, 35, laborer, widower; Garner, Harriet, 26, single, house girl; 18 Jan. 1880; 21 January 1880

Brown, Henry, 26, single, farm hand; Miller, Ann Maria, 19, single, servant; September 1876; 2 October q876

Brown, Henry, 26, single, laborer; Miller, Anne Maria, 19, single, servant; September 1876; 2 October 1876

Brown, Henry, 37, single, laborer; Rasin, Mary E., 27, single, servant; 29 August 1873; 8 December 1873

Brown, Henry, 58, widower, laborer; Bessicks, Annie, 60, widow, cook; 19 June 1873; 25 June 1873

Brown, Isaac, 34, widower, farmhand; Seeney, Henrietta, 18, single, servant; 29 May 1880; 22 April 1880

Brown, Isaiah, 23, single, farmhand; Anderson, Jane, 20, single, servant; 20 October 1876; 26 October 1876

Brown, Isaiah, 23, single, laborer; Johnson, Emma J., 20, single, cook; 28 October 1873; 12 December 1873

Brown, Isaiah, 25, single, farmhand; Anderson, Jane, 20, single, servant; 26 October 1876; 21 October 1876

Brown, James Alfred, 23, single, laborer; Daniels, Mary Francis, 16, single; 10 January 1886; 28 January 1886

Brown, James Alfred, 25, single, farmhand; Wilson, Frances, 19, single, waiter; 16 August1883; 30 August 1883

Brown, James H., 23, widower, farmhand; Matiney, Mary, 19, single, cook; 28 December 1882; 15 January 1883

Brown, James Henry, 23, single, farm hand; Warner, Henrietta, 19, single; 31 December 1876; 10 April 1876

Brown, James Henry, 23, single, farmhand; Warner, Henrietta, 19, single; 31 December 1876; 10 October 1876

Brown, James, 21, single, laborer; Brown, Katie, 18, single, cook; 19 November 1885; 23 December 1885

Brown, James, 22, single, farmhand; Reason, Ella, 18, single, servant; 2 June 1886; 12 June 1886

Brown, James, 30, single, farmhand; Thomas, Elizabeth Jane, 34, single, cook; 6 October 1881; 29 November 1881

Brown, John, 29, single, Laborer; Gardner, Hannah, 25, single; 1 April 1868; 2 June 1868

Brown, Nicholas H., 22, single, laborer; Roner, Mary E., 18 single, servant; 29 January 1880; 17 February 1880

Brown, Nick H., 23, single, laborer; Kever, Emery, 18, single, servant; 28 Jan. 1880; 1 February 1880

Brown, Perry Wilmer, 23, single, farmhand; Jones, Mary, 24, single, cook; 17 December 1882; 9 May 1883

Brown, Perry, 35, single, laborer; Harris, Dinah, 41, widow, washerwoman; 27 May 1880; 12 June 1880

Brown, Thomas, 21, farmhand; Maccon, Susan, 22, seamtress; 17 Oct. 1879; 23 October 1879

Brown, Thomas, 22, single, farmhand; Stanley, Hester Ann, 18, single, cook; 20 Oct. 1881; 10 November 1881

Brown, Upton, 37, single, farmhand; Davis, Ellen, 30, single, widow, cook; 23 July 1882; 17 October 1882

Brown, William A., 22, single, farmhand; Graves, Mary Ann, 18, single; 3 January 1884; 10 January 1883

Brown, William, 29, single, laborer; Hynson, Sarah C., 20, servant, single; 28 Dec. 1867; 9 April 1868

Burns, Richard, 33, farm hand, b. Queen Anne's Co., widower; Miller, Louisa, 22, single, servant; 24 Oct. 1878; 28 October 1878

Butler, Adam, 42, single, laborer; Banks, Rachel, 18, single, cook; 18 December 1873; 24 July 1874

Butler, Alexander, 22, single, laborer; Frisby, Mary, 19, single, servant; 16 May 1883; 15 July 1883

Butler, Alexander, 23, single, laborer; Redding, Mary Elizabeth, 17, single, servant; 30 October 1878; 26 January 1878

Butler, Alexander, 25 widower, farmhand; Chambers, Sarah Elizabeth, 18, single, cook; 5 Jan. 1880; 17 January 1880

Butler, Daniel M.28, single, laborer; Thompson, Frances A., 18, single, servant; 2 March 1871; 7 March 1871

Butler, Daniel, 39, widower, laborer; James, H. A., 35, single, widow, servant; 19 Jan. 1868

Butler, Daniel, 49, widower, farmhand; Smith, Susan, 42, widow, servant; 25 July 1879; 22 April 1880

Butler, Francis, 22, single, laborer; Tanner, Annie, 20, single; 24 September 1870; 16 June 1861

Butler, George D., 22, single, laborer; Jones, Mary J., 20, single, not employed; 25 December 1879; 21 January 1880

Butler, George, 55, widower, farm hand; Chaney, Ann Maria, 35, widow, farm hand; 1 December 1876; 2 October 1876

Butler, George, 55, widower, farmhand; Chaney, Ann Maria, 35, widow, farmhand; 9 December 1876; 2 October 1876

Butler, James P., 21, single, laborer; Thompson, Mary R., 17, single, cook; 29 October 1884; 21 February 1885

Butler, James T., 21, single, laborer; Thompson, Mary R., 17, single, cook; 29 October 1884; 21 February 1885

Butler, James, 24, single, laborer; Thomas, Alethia, 27, single; 6 Oct. 1868; 24 September 1869

Butler, James, 27, single, laborer; Lively, Catherine, 22, single, cook; 20 May 1880; 14 June 1880

Butler, John, 22, single, farmhand; Munson, Belle J., 19 single, cook; 8 September 1884; 8 September 1884

Butler, John, 22, single, farmhand; Munson, Bell J., 19, single, cook; 5 September 1884; 8 September 1884

Butler, Thomas, 24, single, farm hand; Griffin, Sarah Jane, 22, widow, servant; 28 October 1875; 9 December 1875

Butler, Thomas, 24, single, farm hand; Griffin, Sarah Jane, 22, widow, servant; 28 October 1875; 9 December 1875

Butler, William Henry, 24, single, farmhand; Jones, Hannah Liz, 20, single, cook; 9 November 1882; 18 November 1882

Butler, William, 22, single, farmhand; Hodges, Catherine, 21, single, cook; 10 April 1882; 13 April 1882

Butler, William, 22, single, laborer; Frisby, Mary, 19, single, servant; 16 May 1883; 15 July 1884

Cann, Alexander, 22, single, farmhand; Thomas, Annie, 18, single, cook; 20 September 1882; 25 November 1882

Cann, Andrew, 23, single, laborer; Lively, Mary E., 22, single, cook; 20 June 1883; 1 July 1884

Cann, Henry, 22, single, laborer; Redding, Fannie, 21, single, cook; 9 January 1884; 13 May 1884

Cann, Samuel, 25, single, servant; Gooseberry, Martha, 22, single, washerwoman; 19 February 1886; 30 August 1886

Cann, William, 27, single, farmhand; Mitchell, Annie, 16, single, House Girl; 20 July 1882; 27 July 1882

Carmichael, Barney J., 20, single, laborer; White, Rosa C. B., 18, single; 9 June 1886; 10 June 1886

Carmichael, George B., 23, single, fisherman; Johnson, Hattie A., 23, single, cook; 6 July 1882; 14 May 1883

Carmmile, H. I., 21, single, farmhand; Gross, Emma, 22, single, cook; 28 December 1880; 18 January 1881

Carney, Williamm 45, single, farmhand; Bordley, Elizabeth A., 45, widow, cook; 1 October 1884

Carroll, Alfred, 24, single, farmhand; Peaker, Lon, 22, single, cook; 1 December 1880; 25 February 1881

Carroll, Frank, 25, single, farmhand; Baynor, Annie, 27, single, house work; 21 February 1881; 21 February 1881

Carroll, George, single, laborer; Freeman, Rebecca, 20, single, servant; 10 June 1867; 22 June 1867

Carroll, Pere, 21, single, laborer; Scott, Annie, 18, cook, single; 20 September 1883; 13 December 1883

Carroll, Thomas, 23, single, farmhand, New Jersey; Young, Martha E., 21, single; 29 April 1880; 7 May 1880

Carroll, William, 33, single, laborer; Woodland, Annie, 31, widow, servant; 1875; 25 May 1875

Carrow, Francis, 23, single, farmer; Gallison, Martha, 16, single, cook; 7 September 1871; 8 September 1871

Carter, William Henry, 22, single, farmhand; Gross, Harriet C., 20, single, servant; 25 February 1879; 19 January 1880

Carter/Caster, Peter, 41, widower, laborer; Black, Mary Ann, 28; 1867; 14 June 1867

Carver, William, 45, single, laborer; Brown, Mary W., 16, single, servant; 7 July 1886; 17 August 1886

Chambers, G. W., 22, single, laborer; Barroll, Maria, 20, single, servant; 2 February 1870; 16 June 1870

Chambers, George, 37, single, farmhand; Handy, Mary Louise, 38, single, cook; 29 April 1882; 11 May 1882

Chambers, Henry, 38, widower, farmhand; Hynson, Augusta E., 22, single, cook; 21 December 1877; 14 June 1876

Chambers, Horton, 22 1/2, single, lumberman; Blake, Charlotte, 18 3/4, single, servant; 18 May 1875; 10 August 1875

Chambers, James H., 27, single, laborer; Hairston, Anna Maria, 22, single, servant; 31 May 1866; 13 August 1886

Chambers, John, 30, single, farmer; Johnson, Anna, 20, single, servant; 10 April 1871; 21 July 1861

Chambers, John, 46, widower, farmhand; Jones, Minty, 42, single, cook; 25 December 1884; 10 January 1885

Chambers, John, 70, widower, laborer; Trusty, ---, 60, widow, washerwoman; 20 June 1868; 25 June 1868

Chambers, Nathaniel, 35, single, farmhand; Briscoe, Caroline, 30, single, servant; 7 November 1874; 28 December 1874

Chambers, Pere, 29, single, laborer; Jones, Dollie, 16, single, cook; 16 December 1861; 7 August 1872

Chambers, Samuel, 45, single, laborer; Thomas, Mary E., 24, single, servant; 6 September 1866; 8 October 1866

Chambers, William, 62, widower, farmhand; Miles, Hester Ann, 61, widow, cook; 20 December 1883; 25 June 1884

Chaney, Alexander, 45, single, laborer; Carroll, Elizabeth, 38, single, cook; 17 July 1885; 21 February 1885

Chapman, Arthur, 25, single, laborer; Trusty, Jane, 25, single, cook; 14 June 1868; 2 January 1869

Chase, James H., 24, widower, laborer; Hopkins, Harriet, 22, single, cook; 25 April 1883; 25 April 1883

Chatman, Charles H., 21, single, laborer; Whittington, Emeline, 18, single; 29 March 1868; 10 August 1868

Chatman, William Thomas, 35, single, laborer; Oakley, Mary Ann, 18, single, servant; 16 May 1883; 13 December 1883

Chigunters, Charles, 27, farmhand, single; Kennard, Margaret, 21, single, servant; 1 May 1877; 17 May 1877

Christy, William Alfred, 24, single; Munson, Georgiannna, 21, single; 3 January 1884; 4 April 1884

Clark, Charles H., 58, widower, farmhand; Bowen, Mary A., 45, widow, housekeeper; 24 September 1885; 2 October 1885

Clark, Emory James, 25, single, farmhand; Harris, Mary Jane, 23, single, cook; 8 September 1876

Clarkson, Alexander, 23, single, farmhand; Pearce, Elizabeth, 22, single, cook; 31 August 1880; 11 September 1880

Clayton, George W., 21, single, laborer; Freeman, Editha, 18, single, servant; 18 February 1869; 26 July 1869

Clayton, Henry, 25, single, farmhand; Butler, Ellen, 30, widow, house servant; 20 October 1876; 28 October 1876

Clayton, James, 24, single, laborer; Roleters, Sarah R., 21, single, servant; 2 August 1866; 7 February 1867

Cole, Robert L., 19, single, farmhand; Rasin, Mary E., 20, single, cook; 4 January 1883; 14 May 1883

Collins, James E., 27, single, farmhand; Wilmer, Mary E., 27, single, cook; 28 February 1884; 8 March 1884

Comegys, Alexander, 29, single, laborer; Freeman, Laura Jane, 26, single, cook; 3 May 1877; 21 August 1877

Comegys, Ben, 22, single, farmhand; Stevens, Mamie, 18, single; 24 July 1884; 31 July 1884

Comegys, Benjamin, 50, widower, farmhand; Butler, Henrietta, 40, single, cook; 18 February 1886; 30 August 1886

Comegys, George, 21, single, laborer; Bowser, Mary, 24, single, cook; 30 December 1885; 15 January 1886

Comegys, George, 22, single, farmhand Recorded in Liber DCB; Brown, Julia, 18, single, houseworker; 10 June 1878; 18 June 1878

Comegys, George, 23, widower, laborer; Brown, Mary, 16, single, house girl; 25 December 1879; 5 May 1880

Comegys, John H, 24, single, farmhand; Thompson, Louisa, 22, single, servant; 28 December 1876

Comegys, Robert, 21, single, laborer; Dennings, Marianna, 20, single; 27 February1868; 25 June 1868

Comegys, William, 38, single, farmhand; Roulette, Temperence, 21, single, servant; 16 November 1876; 3 February 1877

Cooper, Benjamin, 42, widower, farmhand; Hynson, Letitia, 43m widow, cook; 8 January 1885; 10 January 1885

Cooper, Isaac, 23, single, farmhand; Graves, Georgeanna, 21, single, domestic; 14 May 1874; 25 May 1874

Cooper, Jacob Henry, 27, farmhand; Vickerson, Violena, 25, single, cook; 12 January 1882; 28 January 1882

Cooper, John Henry, 24, single, farmhand; Thomas, Mary Jane, 18, cook, single; 18 September 1879; 22 April 1880

Cooper, Louis, 46, widower, laborer; Demby, Margaret, 27, single; 15 February 1868; 14 March 1868

Cooper, Robert, 26, single, farmhand; Mitchell, Lena, 21, widow, cook; 25 May 1882; 12 July 1882

Cooper, Robert, 31, widower, farmhand; Chambers, Annie, 22, single, cook; 4 May 1886; 19 May 1886

Cooper, William H., 30, single, laborer; Sanders/Saunders, Henrietta, 39, widow; 26 August 1869; 16 June 1870

Cooper, Zachariah, 28 single, farmhand; Wilson, Editha, 20, single, cook; 6 May 1880; 7 September 1880

Cord(?), James Thomas, 30, widower, laborer; --------, Harriett Ann, 28, widow, servant; 13 December 1871; 7 August 1872

Corse, Alexander, 21, single, laborer; Morocco, Lydia A., 20, single, cook; 5 September 1870; 16 June 1871

Corsey, Corsey, 24, single, laborer; Jenkins, Elizabeth, 28, single, cook; 25 September 1879; 22 April 1880

Cotton, Abram, 48, single, widower; Ward, Sarah, 21, single, servant; 14 October 1869; 6 June 1870

Cotton, Alfred, 37, single, farmhand; Blake, Sarah, 45, widow, cook; 20 January 1876; 21 August 1877

Cotton, George, 21, single, laborer; Rasin, Annie, 21, single, domestic; 25 December 1873; 31 December 1873

Cotton, Henry H., 23, single, farmhand; Comegys, Harriet, 23, single, cook; 9 September 1880; 11 November 1880

Cotton, Isaac Joseph, 22, single, laborer; Green, Francis, 21, single, cook; 13 April 1873; 2 May 1873

Cotton, John B., 31, single, waiter; Brown, Mary E., 18, single, cook; 19 October 1870; 24 October 1870

Cotton, John, 23, single, farmhand; Huston, Rachael, 42, cook; 12 October 1885; 14 December 1885

Cotton, Samuel, 50, single, laborer; Harris, Dinah, 50, single, cook; 31 July 1884; 28 August 1884

Covington, William H., 41, widower, laborer; Brown, Jane, 33, widow, cook; 15 March 1883; 1 May 1883

Coxson, Perry, 25, single, farmhand; Bright, Caroline, 23, single, cook; 25 March 1880; 1 April 1880

Crossley, 31, single, widower; Elliott, Mary Eliza, 22, single; 29 January 1868; 14 March 1868

Crossley, Moses, 70, widower, farmhand; Barney, Elizabeth, 65, widow, cook; 1881; 21 February 1881

Davis, Henry, 22, single, farmhand; Duman/Doman, Mary E., 24, single, cook; 6 June 1870; 11 June 1870

Davis, Henry, 47, widower, plasterer; Hall, Louisa, 27, single, domestic; 9 June 1874; 28 December 1874

Davis, Henry, single, laborer; Chambers, Betsy, widow, servant; 1 June 1868; 16 January 1869

Davis, John, 28, widower, laborer; Thomas, Irene, 18, single; 6 August 1869; 22 December 1869

Davis, Peter, 47, single, laborer; Augustus, Eliza Jane, 37, servant; 23 June 1881; 3 September 1881

Day, Bostow, 40, single, farmhand; Cotton, Sely Maria, 21; 21 July 1881; 26 August 1881

Dellyha, Peter, 46, widower, sailor; Gray, Eliza, servant; 9 December 1881; 14 March 1882

Demby, George, 28, single, laborer; Plater, Louisa, 32, single, servant; 18 February 1869; 26 July 1869

Dent, John, 30, single, sailor; Gray, Fannie, 27, single, cook; 15 October 1870; 17 October 1870

Derry, David, 20, single, laborer; Graves, Joanna, 18, single; 25 August 1868; 5 November 1868

Derry, Josiah, 21, single, farmhand; Graves, Mary E., 18, single, cook; 29 December 1870; 3 March 1871

Derry, Josiah, 36, widower, farmhand; Barroll, Elizabeth, 38, single, cook; 3 December 1885; 14 December 1885

Derry, Theodore, 45, widower, farmhand; Brown, Caroline, 36, widow, cook; 5 November 1881; 4 January 1882

Derry, Wesley, 25, single, farmhand; Jones, Ella, 18, single, cook; 31 December 1884; 3 January 1885

Dien/Dier, John, 42, widower, laborer; Morlock, Annie, 35, widow, cook; 26 December 1879; 19 January 1880

Doman, Daniel, 29, single, laborer; Biddle, Hannah, 23 single, housemaid; 1867; 14 June 1867

Doman, David, 32, single, farmer; Rasin, Ann, 29, widow; 13 April 1872; 15 April 1872

Doran, James A., 23, single, laborer; Wilson, Kate, 22, single, servant; 28 December 1868; 24 September 1869

14

Dorsey, Alexander, 22, single, farmhand; Tilghman, Rosetta, 18, single, cook; 21 February 1885

Dorsey, James, 22, single, sailor; Reese, Elizabeth, 19, single, cook; 20 January 1879; 19 January 1880

Dorsey, John Thomas, 22, single, farmhand; Brunswick, Florence, 17, single, servant; 14 May 1879; 17 May 1879

Dorsey, John W., 22, single, farmhand; Hance, Ella N., single, cook; 15 February 1883; 9 May 1883

Dorsey, John. 22, single, farmhand; Morgan, Hattie, 25, single, cook; 26 December 1883; 31 March 1884

Dorsey, Perry Henry, 23, single, farmhand; Gale, ___ M., 19, single, cook; 10 January 1878; 26 January 1878

Douglass, William, 30, single, farmhand; Meridth, Henrietta, 22, widow, cook; 27 December 1876; 3 February 1877

Downes, James E., 39, single, laborer; Handy, Fanny, 22, single, cook; 14 January 1884; 8 February 1884

Downs, John, 22, single, farmhand; Murray, Maria, 20, single, cook; 31 December 1882; 1 May 1883

Draper, John, 22, single, laborer; Matthews, Ophelia, 22, single, servant; 2 April 1868; 10 August 1868

Dudley, Charles, 21, single, farmhand; Jones, Marion, 18, single, cook; 23 December 1884; 1 January 1885

Dudley, John F, 24, single, laborer; Murray, Catherine, 18, single, servant; 17 December 1873; 24 December 1875

Dudley, John, 26, single, farmhand; Clayton, Georgianna, 22, widow, cook; 28 May 1884; 17 December 1884

Dudley, Manuel, 30, single, farmhand; Black, Hester, 20, single; 12 December 1879; 19 March 1879

Dullum, Daniel, 32, single, laborer; Granger, Annie, 38, widow, cook; 13 May 1886; 14 May 1886

Dunn, Alfred, 25, single, laborer; Mander, Mary Ellen, 22; 19 April 1881; 31 March 1881

Dunn, William Alfred, 28, widower, farmhand; Kennard, Jennie E., 23, single, cook; 11 October 1883; 18 October 1883

Dunn, William S., 40, widower, farmer; Brown, Caroline, single, servant; 7 May 1872; 25 June 1873

Dunn, William, 52, widower, fisherman; Smith, Anna, 25, single, cook; 13 October 1884; 5 November 1884

Dy__, John, 51, single; Griffin, Julia, 44, single; 18 April 1883; 20 April 1883

Edwards, John F., 23, single, laborer; Chambers, Hannah, 18, single, cook; 15 September 1870; 16 September 1870

Elias, Henry, 30, single, farmhand; Frisby, Julia, 35, widow, cook; 20
April 1881; 25 March 1882
Emory, Moses, 23, single, farmhand; Harris, Mary E., 18, single; 29
April 1883; 29 May 1883
Fields, John, 25, single, farmhand; Grommes, Elizabeth, 18, servant; 25
September 1876; 2 October 1876
Fields, John, 29, widower, farmhand; Graves, Maria, 25, single,
housework; 12 October 1880; 13 October 1880
Fisher, George Washington, 30, single, laborer; Hackett, Isabella, 23,
single; 16 September 1873
Fisher, William, 52, widower, laborer; Arthur, Millicent, 52, widow,
House servant; 3 February 1866; 16 February 1866
Fletcher, George W. 44, single, farmhand; Anderson, Martha, 40, single,
cook; 31 March 1880; 1 April 1880
Fletcher, John F., 23, single, merchant; Perkins, Anna M., 28, single; 1
July 1872; 5 September 1872
Floyd, James, 25, single, farmhand; Graves, Tempy, 25, single,
seamstress; 6 August 1885; 10 August 1885
Floyd, Thomas, 28, single, teamster; Woolford, Elizabeth, 39, widow; 5
December 1882
Floyd, William, 21, single, laborer; Wilmer, Annie, 20, single, cook; 20
April 1873
Ford, Alexander, 39, widower, farmhand; Walley, Catherine, 32, widow,
cook; 7 April 1885; 20 April 1851
Ford, Emmett, 23, single, farmhand; Harkless, Sas__, 17, single; 14
March 1885; 22 April 1885
Ford, Emory, 26, single, farmhand; Wells, Louisa, 21, single, cook; 1
October 1881
Ford, Emory, 26, single, farmhand; Berryman, Mary, 21, single, cook; 15
October 1884; 15 January 1884
Ford, Feorge Washington, 21, single, farmhand; Starling, Florence, 18,
single, cook; 12 September 1878; 16 November 1878
Ford, George W., 22, single, farmhand; Seney, Lydia _, 23, single,
servant; 1875
Ford, John H., 26, single, farmhand; Starling, Anna L., 18, single, cook;
9 May 1883
Ford, John Wesley, 22, single, farmhand; Starling, Mary Louise, 18,
single; 27 July 1880; 29 July 1880
Ford, William H, 26, single, farmhand; Ambert, Georgianna, 24, single,
cook; 20 May 1880; 15 June 1880
Ford, William, 25, single, laborer; Hynson, Louisa, 20, single, servant;
10 February 1870; 7 October 1870

Fowler, Jacob, 35, single, laborer; Wilson, Lizzie, 25, single, cook; 27 November 1884; 30 January 1885

Franklin, Peter, 28, single, farmhand; Wiggins, Susan, 18, single, cook; 9 January 1884

Freeman, Alexander, 48, widower, laborer; Towson, Lizzie Ann, 17, single, servant; 28 November 1870; 21 July 1871

Freeman, Benjamin J., 22, single, farmhand; Lively, Anna Maria, 21, single, cook; 14 November 1881

Freeman, Benjamin, 21, single, farmhand; Kennard, Elizabeth, 19, single, cook; 9 May 1883

Freeman, Charles H., 23, single, laborer; Mander, Sally, 15, single; 9 February 1870; 22 March 1870

Freeman, Charles H., 28, widower, farmhand; Johnson, Elizabeth, 30, single, cook; 29 December 1883

Freeman, Perry, 21, single, laborer; Wallis, Lizzie, 16, single, servant; 29 July 1869; 16 June 1870

Frisby, Caromile, 22, laborer, Queen Anne's Co; Montgomery, Eleanor, single; June 1867; 16 June 1867

Frisby, Charles, 22, single, farmhand; Roberts, Mintie, 19 single, cook; 14 November 1881

Frisby, George, 51, widower, laborer; White, Clarissa Ann, 38; 24 December 1874; 9 May 1883

Frisby, Henry, 35, single, farmhand; Miller, Sallie, 30, single, servant; 4 May 1878; 20 June 1878

Frisby, James, 30, widower, servant; Butcher, Sallie, 18, widow, servant; 21 December 1868; 8 January 1869

Frisby, Michael, widower, butcher; Johnson, Maria, 17, single; 12 February 1868; 25 June 1868

Frisby, William, 25, single, laborer; James, Jane, 30, single, housekeeper; 20 September 1870; 21 July 1871

Gaddess, James H. H. 25, single, laborer; Freeman, Rebecca, 23, single, housekeeper; 9 September1867; 14 March 1868

Gale, Philip, 42, widower, laborer; Gordon, Maria, 19, single, servant; 31 October 1871; 18 March 1882

Gale, Richard. 23,widower, oysterman; Berry, Eliza Ann, single, servant; 19 December 1860; 7 April 1869

Ganes, Samuel, 25, single, laborer, Hanover Co. Virginia; Butler, Jane, 20, single, servant; 27 May 1868; 9 June 1868

Garner, Horace, 23, single, laborer; Dorsey, Mary, 23, single, servant; 25 October 1876; 28 October 1876

Garnett, George, 26, single, cook; Cotton, Helen, 22, single, cook; 31 December 1885; 13 August 1886

Garrison, Abraham, 30, single, laborer; Miller, Mary Louisa, 26, widow, cook; 15 July 1883; 12 February 1884

Garrison, Jacob, 30, single, farm laborer; Hall, Harriet E. 20, single, servant; 26 September 1877; 16 March 1878

Garrison, James _, 25, single, laborer; Buckner, Mary C., 22, single, cook; 29 December 1881; 4 January 1882

Garrison, John H., 37, widower, laborer; Bright, Sarah E., widow, servant; 23 December 1871; 25 June 1873

Garrison, John, 26, single, laborer; Wilson, Isabella, 23, single; 22 August 1868; 24 September 1868

Garrison, Johnson, 29, widower, farmhand; Brown, Martha, 25, single, cook; 3 January 1879

Garrison, William Henry, 37, widower, laborer; Hopkins, Martha E., 28, single, cook; 23 December 1872; 5 March 1873

Garrison, William Wesley, 32, single, farmhand; Demby, Francis Jane, 19, single, servant; 31 May 1876; 3 February 1877

Gibbs, James 40, widower, farmhand; Butcher, Sarah Ann, 23, single, servant; December 1874; 21 January 1876

Gibbs, James, 25, single, farmhand; Cork, Ella, 25, single; 23 October 1879; 27 October 1879

Gibbs, Joseph, 22, single, farmhand; Sanders, Jane L., 19, single; 18 April 1881; 23 April 1881

Gibbs, Joseph, 25, single, farmhand; Massey, Mary, 20, single, domestic; 27 October 1881; 2 February 1883

Gibbs, Joshua, 22, widower, laborer; Stewart, Susan, 20, single, cook; 28 August 1873; 6 May 1874

Gibbs, Stephen, 26, single, factory hand; Watson, Ella, 16, single, servant; 16 August 1880; 25 February 1881

Gilbert, Henry, 27, single, oysterman; Thomas, Sarah E., 26, single; 22 December 1868; 2 January 1869

Givens, Silas, 21, single, laborer; Kennard, Harriet, 22, single, servant; 28 December 1876; 2 February 1877

Gland, Jeremiah, 22, single, laborer; Johnson, Margaret, 18, single, servant; 23 December 1869; 16 June 1870

Gleaves, Charles H., 24, single, farmhand; Chambers, Alice, 18, single, cook; 7 November 1882; 18 November 1882

Gleaves, Edward, 26, single, farmhand; Francis, Mary, 18, single, cook; 30 November 1884; 30 January 1885

Gleaves, Elijah, 22, single, farmhand; Price, Mary, 28, widow, servant; 2 June 1879; 10 July 1879

Gleaves, Isaac, 24, single, farmhand; Carroll, Nellie, 20, single, cook; 11 May 1884; 12 May 1884

Gleaves, Pere S, 23, single, laborer; Ferrell, Margaret, 19, single, servant; 6 January 1874; 6 May 1874

Gleaves, Primus, 23, single, laborer; Comegys, Charlotte, 25, single, servant; 29 September 1870; 21 July 1871

Gleeves, Samuel, 22, single, farmhand; Brown, Annie E., 18, single, cook; 29 May 1882

Glenn, Charles W., 26, single, laborer; Thompson, Mary L., 18, single, cook; 30 December 1883; 15 July 1884

Glenn, Houston, 30, single, laborer; Wilson, Annie F., 20, single, cook; 8 December 1870

Glenn, Levi, 30, single, laborer; Murray, Martha, single, servant; 22 June 1867; 7 April 1869

Good, Nicholas, 18, single, laborer; Cooper, Jane E., 22, single, house servant; 29 January 1866; 17 October 1866

Gooding, Pere, 23, single, farmhand; Scott, Adeline, 22, single, servant; 14 February 1879; 22 April 1880

Gordon, Isaac M., 28, single, farmhand; Hutchins, Teresa, 20, single; 23 June 1876; 20 December 1876

Gordon, John Wesley, 23, single, waiter; Mitchell, Alverta, 18, single, nurse; 26 December 1882; 14 May 1883

Gosman, Henry, 26, single, carpenter; Campbell, Alethia, 18, milliner; 5 April 1883; 13 April 1883

Gould, James, 65, laborer; Thomas, Sarah, 30, single, servant; 4 December 1873; 8 December 1873

Granger, Charles Henry, 22, single, teamster; Cooper, Hester, 18, single, cook; 1877; 1 April 1880

Granger, Isaac, 63, widower, laborer; Scott, Betsy, 65, widow, cook; 7 September 1872; 25 June 1873

Granger, Isaac, 63, widower, laborer; Scott, Betsy, 65, widow, cook; 7 September 1872; 25 June 1873

Granger, Isaac, 65, widower, farmhand; Carroll, Annie, 35, single, cook; 17 February 1880; 19 July 1880

Granger, James E., 24, single, carter; Jenkins, Alice, 25, single, cook; 23 November 1882; 14 May 1883

Graves, Aaron, 22, widower, laborer; Jones, Annie, 23, single; 21 November 1872(Baltimore, Md.); 256 June 1873

Graves, Emory, 28, single, farmhand; Yorker, Mary Elizabeth, 26, single, servant; 28 June 1876; 25 October 1876

Graves, Emory, 35, single, laborer; Chambers, Lidie, 33, widow, cook; 24 November1885; 15 December 1885

Graves, Filmore, 24, single, farmhand; Frisby, Margaret, 18, single; 4 September 1880; 12 December 1880

Graves, George E., 40, widower, farmhand; Hastings, Jane R., 35, widow, cook; 28 February 1884; 11 March 1884

Graves, George, 21, single, laborer; Griffin, Louisa, 30, single, servant; 22 December 1869; 3 March 1871

Graves, George, 25, single, farmhand; Wright, Rachel, 22, single, house girl; 4 January 1883; 12 June 1883

Graves, George, 32, widower, farmhand; Brown, Milly, 34, widow, cook; 18 August 1881; 10 November 1881

Graves, Henry, 24, single, farming; White, Edie E., 18, single, cook; 6 November 1877; 26 January 1878

Graves, Henry, 40, laborer; Meeds, Martha, 22, house servant; 26 February 1866/1 March 1866; 17 October 1866

Graves, Hyde, 30, single, farmhand; Duckery, Mary F., 28, single, cook; 8 October 1885; 9 October 1885

Graves, James H., 32, single, laborer; Groves, Milley, 21, single, house servant; 31 April 1866; 13 August 1866

Graves, James S., 23, single, laborer; Houston, Sarah E., 26, single, cook; 3 January 1873; 25 June 1873

Graves, John E., 26, single, laborer; Stewart, Mary E., 20, cook, single; 3 March 1871

Graves, John E., 35, widower, farmhand; Gilbert, Melissa, 34, widow, cook; 20 December 1881; 26 February 1884

Graves, John Marshall, 25, single, farmhand; Rogers, Polly Ann, 18, single, cook; 5 June 1876; 12 December 1876

Graves, John, 23, single, laborer; Yorker, Louise, 19, single, servant; 6 November 1873

Graves, Levi R. 24, single, laborer; Thomas, Margaret, 22, single, cook; 22 April, 1880; 14 June 1880

Graves, William, 30, single, plasterer; Bradshaw, Debie, 45, widow; 18 November 18__; 27 May 1875

Green, Richard, 22, single, farmhand; Carroll, Mary, 19, single, servant; 15 June 1879; 1 June 1879

Green, Samuel, 38, widower, laborer; Collins, Sarah, 25, widow, servant; 5 January 1875; 27 May 1875

Greenage, Henry, 24, single, farmhand; Wilson, Elizabeth, 21, single, cook; 7 June 1881; 3 September 1881

Greenfield, William, 37, single, farmer; Brown, Lizzie B., 25, single, cook; 6 June 1878; 12 May 1878

Griffin, Charles W. H., 25, single, farmhand; Smith, Deborah A., 25, single, cook; 7 October 1880; 19 October 1880

Griffin, John H., 28, single, farmhand; Thompson, Martha I., 26, single, cook; 20 January 1881; 20 January 1881

Griffith, James. 24, single, farmhand; Sheppard, Editha, 26, single, cook; 16 February 1882; 18 February 1882

Griffith, Samuel, 27, single, farmer; Reed, Sarah, 17, single, cook; 22 April 1880

Griner, Alexander, 33, single, farmhand; Kellum, Rosie, 26, single, cook; 24 May1880; 14 June 1880

Groom, John, 40, widower, farmhand; Johnson, Matilda, 44, widow, cook; 31 December 1878; 3 January 1879

Groome, John, 21, single, farmhand; Lyle, Sallie, 17, single; 17 March 1881; 10 March 1881

Groomes, John W, 21, single, laborer; Wailes, Robertine, 16, single, cook; 25 June 1872

Grooms, John W., 33, widower, farmhand; Doman, Harriet, 22, single, cook; 2 September 1885; 9 November 1885

Grooms, John, 25, single, farmhand; Chaney, Mary, 16, single; 15 May 1879; 22 April 1880

Hackett, Anthony, 24, single, farmhand; Spencer, Emily L., 22, single; 25 December 1878; 27 December 1878

Hackett, Charles T., 28, single, farmhand; Saunders, Florence, 18, single; 25 August 1881; 21 February 1881

Hackett, George C., 23, single, laborer; Dunn, Annie V., 18, single, cook; 5 January 1880; 22 April 1880

Hackett, James, 21, single, farmhand; Elbert, Tempy, 25, single, servant; 4 September 1879; 27 October 1879

Hackett, Samuel, 16, single, single, farmhand; Butler, Georgianna, 16, single, domestic; 15 November 1876; 14 June 1877

Hales, William, 25, single, laborer; Blake, Anna Maria, 18, servant; 1868; 25 June 1868

Hall, George H., 24, single, farmhand; Jones, Lizzie, 18, single, cook; 10 August 1880; 7 June 1881

Hall, John, 28, single, laborer; Ford, Margaret, 21, single; 28 May 1874; 31 December 1874

Hamilton, B. A. Jr., 26, single, farmhand; Granger, Lizzie, 23, single, cook; 23 September 1881; 14 November 1881

Hammond, Jervis, 37, widower, farmhand; Tilghman, Caroline, 32, widow, cook; 16 November 1881; 18 November 1881

Hampton, John, 20, single, laborer; Massey, Lydia, 22, single, servant; 14 October 1869; 16 October 1869

Handy, Samuel, 28, laborer; Pennick, Emily, 24, single, servant; 1873; 15 November 1873

Handy, Samuel, 28, single, laborer; Bennick/Pennick, Emily, 24, single, servant; 1873; 25 November 1873

Hanson, James H., 40, single, laborer; Garrison, Mary E., 24, single, servant; 19 August 1869; 22 December 1869

Hanson, J. Thomas, single, laborer; Anderson, Mary E., single; 26 January 1871; 16 June 1871

Hardin, William H., 30, widower, farmhand; Jones, Mary E., 26, single, cook; 22 September 1880; 1 October 1880

Harding, Stephen, single, laborer; Trusty, Anna M., single; 31 December 1871; 19 January 1872

Harding, William H., 22, single, laborer; Ringgold, Laura, 20, single, cook; 27 December 1871; 21 July 1871

Harris, Abram, 22, single, farmhand; Scott, Lucy, 25, single, servant; 5 October 1882; 14 November 1882

Harris, Isaac, 21, single, farmhand; Smith, Welthy, 18, single, cook; 19 May 1884; 28 May 1884

Harris, Isaac, 30, widower, farmhand; Barlow, Emma, 24, single, servant; 11 September 1873; 10 April 1884

Harris, Jacob, 24, single, laborer; Anderson, Mary, 20, single, cook; 7 October 1871; 22 January 1872

Harris, Jacob, 24, single, laborer; Anderson, Mary, 20, single, cook; 7 October 1871; 22 January 1872

Harris, James, 22, single, farmhand; Brown, Nancy, 20, single, cook; 3 June 1880; 4 June 1880

Harris, John, 24, single, farmhand; Turner, Lizzie, 21, single, cook; 5 September 1884; 15 November 1884

Harris, Joseph, 36, single, laborer; Blake, Sally, 27, single, servant; 15 September 1866; 9 August 1867

Harris, Richard, 22, single, farmhand; Hynson, Francis, 19, single; 26 December 1878; 31 December 1878

Harris, Robert, 25, single, laborer; Green, Alice, 20, single, servant; 7 June 1867; 22 June 1867

Harris, Samuel, 25, single, farmhand; Brown, Emily Ann, 23, single, servant; 6 January 1875; 15 March 1875

Harris, Shadrach, 65, widower, farmhand; Lindsey, Chloe A., 55, widow, housekeeper; 27 December 1883; 29 June 1883

Harris, William H., 22, single, laborer; Anderson, Louisa, 19, single, servant; 24 December 1867; 25 June 1868

Harris, William H., 28, single, farmhand; Blackburn, Margaret A., 24, single, servant; 3 December 1885; 4 December 1885

Harris, William, 21, single, laborer; Nichols, Rachel I., 29, single, cook; 13 June 1867; 14 June 1867

Harrison, Emanuel, 22, single, laborer; Munson, Henrietta, 24, single, servant; 7 December 1875; 15 March 1875

Hastings, George. 23, single, laborer; Butler, Lizzie, 21, single, servant; 6 April 1869; 24 September 1869

Hatton, George, 28, single, farmhand; Wilson, Harriet Ann, 22, single, cook; 1 January 1882; 2 January 1882

Hazell, Charles, 35, single, sailor; Garrison, Kate, 27, single, cook; 30 April 1884; 13 May 1884

Helmsley, Risdon E., 26, single, laborer; Brooks, Lizzie, 22, single, cook; 27 December 1882; 2 February 1883

Hemsley, Leroy/Percy, 27, single, laborer; Davis, Jane, 17, single; 15 April 1868; 10 August 1868

Henry, George R., 22, single, laborer; Ward, Catherine, 17, single, cook; 30 September 1872; 30 September 1872

Henry, George R., 22, single, laborer; Ward, Catherine, 17,single, cook; 30 September 1872; 30 September 1872

Henry, Isaac, 19, single, laborer; Moore, Julia A., single; 20 November1872; 25 June 1873

Henry, Isaac, 19, single, laborer; Moore, Julia A., single, cook; 28 November 1872; 25 June 1873

Herbert, George A., 28, single, laborer; Philips, Nancy J., 18, single, cook; 29 December 1881; 4 January 1882

Hewes, James. 24, single, farmer; Brown, Ellen, 22, single, servant; 11 July 1872; 25 September 182

Hicks, Thomas, 22, single, labroer; Freeman, Martha, single; 23 December 1868; 2 January 1869

Hicks, Thomas, 27, widower, farmhand; Burgen, Maria, 37, widow, servant; 18 December 1875; 21 December 1875

Hill, David, 26, single, laborer; Frisby, Rachel, 22, single, cook; 19 January 1864; 6 May 1874

Hill, William Edward, 24, single, laborer; Rasin, Victoria, 23, widow, cook; 26 August 1876; 11 September 1876

Hill, William, 35, single, farmhand; Williams, Nancy, 32, single, cook; 8 April 1880; 9 April 1880

Hinson, Henry, 23, single, farmhand; Maddon, Charlotte, 24, single, cook; 16 January 1877; 30 January 1877

Hodges, Clarence, 21, single, laborer; Frisby, Lavinia, 17, single, cook; 18 May 1880; 22 April 1880

Hodges, James, 30, single, laborer; Kennard, Jane, 30, widow, servant; 24 October 1868; 22 December 1869

Hodges, Louis, 23, single, farmhand; Brice, Rosa, 25, widow, cook; 15 January 1879; 22 April 1880

Hodges, Richard, 25, single, farmer; Johnson, Mary D., 20, single, servant; 12 February 1869; 7 April 1869

Hodges, Theodore, 21, single, farmhand; Scott, Matilda, 22, single, cook; 4 October 1883; 31 March 1884

Hodges, Pere, 30, single, farmhand; Thomas, Julia, 19, single, cook; 4 March 1880; 14 November 1880

Holland, Solomon E., 20, single, farmhand; Daniels, Henrietta, 38, widow; 25 June 1874

Hollins, John R., 24, single, farmhand; Worrell, Mary Ann, 19, single; 12 August 1876; 25 October 1876

Hollins, George, single, farmhand; Murray, Jane, 18, single, cook; 10 August 1880; 27 August 1881

Homely, James H., 44, widower, farmhand; Gardener, Harriett, 30, widow, servant; 29 December 1879; 5 January 1880

Hopkins, C. H., 25, single, laborer; Massey, Mary, 20, single; 23 November1867; 5 March 1868

Hopkins, George G., 33, single, barber; Wright, Mary Ellen, 35, single, cook; 3 January 1883; 18 June 18883

Horsey, Charles A., 30, widower, clergyman; Brown, Mary E., 17, single, domestic; 29 October 1876; 10 October 1876

Houston, Daniel Jacob, 25, single, farmhand; Bargus, Adeline 30, widow, cook; 4 August 1879; 28 August 1879

Houston, Handy, 42, single, farmhand; Mander, Sallie, 40, widow, cook, 12 July 1880; July 1880; 13 July 1880

Howard, Andrew, 40, widower, farmhand; Ringgold, Annie, 25, single, cook; 10 April 1886; 30 August 1886

Howes, Jacob, 23, single, sailor; Gorman, Lizzie, 21, single, cook; 13 April 1870; 17 April 1870

Hull, John H., 21, single, farmhand; Fletcher, Georgianna, 18, single, servant; 3 June 1886; 5 June 1886

Hurley, Samuel H; Merchant, Alice; 4 October 1866; 9 October 1866

Hurley, William, 27, single, laborer; Raisin, Julia, 27, single, servant; 29 December 1866; 17 October 1866

Hurtt, George W., single, laborer; Brown, Sarah L; 27 August 1867; 29 August 1867

Hurtt, George, 34, single, farmhand; Johnson, Clara, 21, single, nurse; 25 December 1872; 5 January 1884

Hurtt, John, 38, single, farmer; Postman, Sarah L., 27, single, servant; 22 August 1878; 26 August 1878

Hurtt, Samuel C., 21, single, farmhand; Russell, Mary E., 21, single, cook; 14 October 1880; 19 October 1880

Hurtt, Thomas J., 53, widower, farmhand; Richards, Eliza D., 50, single, teacher; 6 May 1880; 13 July 1880

Hutchins, Barney, 46, widower, laborer; Walker, Mary, 28, single, servant; 29 July 1870

Hynson, Amos, single, laborer; Spencer, M. A., 18, single, servant; 11
    January 1867; 5 May 1868
Hynson, Charles H., 35, single, farmhand; Frisby, Caroline, 32, widow;
    27 August 1878; 4 January 1879
Hynson, Emory, 30, laborer, single; Ringgold, Amanda, 25, single,
    servant; 23 November 1865; 23 January 1866
Hynson, Henry, 20, single, farmhand; Johnson, Mary, 19, single, cook,
    Queen Anne's Co; 3 October 1883; 30 October 1883
Hynson, Isaac H., 23, single, farmhand; Hynson, Mary Jane, 19, single,
    cook; 26 May 1874; 2 August 1874
Hynson, James W., 23, single, farmhand; Wilson, Margaret, 21, single,
    cook; 8 April 1886; 19 May 1886
Hynson, Jervis, 23, single, farmhand; Scott, Carolyn, 22, single, servant;
    19 November 1874; 24 July 1875
Hynson, Richard, 45, widower, farmhand; Reed, Mary, 45, widow; 17
    September 1880; 20 September 1881
Hynson, William, 24, single, laborer; Sanders, Rachel, 18, single, cook; 3
    June 1872; 23 June 1873
Hynson, William, 24, single, laborer; Sanders, Rachel, 18, single, cook; 3
    June 1872; 23 June 1873
Irving, Louis H., 25, single, farmhand; Riley, Martha J., 19, single, house
    girl; 1 July 1880; 1 July 1880
Jackson, Edward, 26, single, laborer; Poice, Hannah E., 24, single,
    servant; 7 June 1873; 6 May 1874
Jackson, John Quincy Adams, 25, single, laborer; Tanner, Amanda, 21,
    single, servant; 26 December 1865; 26 December 1865
Jackson, Louis A., 26, single, farmhand; Williams, Lizzie, 17, single,
    cook; 19 May 1886; 20 May 1886
Jackson, Samuel, 27, widower, laborer; Spencer, Mary E., 18, single,
    cook; 26 April 1874; 31 December 1874
Jackson, William, 20, single, farmhand; Miller, Mary Ellen, 18, single;
    13 June 1867; 24 April 1869
James, Grinage H., 25, single, farmhand; Johnson, Jane H., 18, single,
    servant; 28 November 1876; 10 October 1876
James, Levi, 23, single, farmhand; Comegys, Hannah, 17, single; 3
    August 1882; 6 September 1882
James, William, 22, single, laborer; Jones, Sarah Elizabeth, 19, single,
    servant; 1 June 1871; 18 September 1871
Jeffers, Albert, 25, single, farmer; Rickett, Sarah, 24, single, cook; 6
    January 1886; 16 March 1886
Jeffers, J. Wesley, 24, widower, farmhand; Turner, Martha, 22, single,
    cook; 2 August 1878; 22 April 1880

Jeffries, Daniel, 22, single, farmhand; Redding, Martha, 21, widow, cook; 7 May 1884; 21 February 1885

Jeffries, Joseph, 55, widower, laborer; Frazier, Ann E., 43, widow, servant; 2 June 1874; 23 December 1874

Jenkins, Nathaniel, 25, single, laborer; Frisby, Ann Rebecca, 24, single, servant; 2 January 1872; 10 July 1872

Jesco, James, 28, single, oysterman; Wright, Eliza, 24, single, servant; 31 December 1876; 10 April 1876

Johns, Emory, 27, single, laborer; Johnson, Lucy Ann, 20, single; 1 April 1868; 2 June 1868

Johnson, Alexander, 27, single, laborer; Anderson, Caroline, 16, single, cook; 16 June 1868; 16 January 1869

Johnson, Alfred W., 23, single, laborer; Wright, Emily, 16, single, domestic, Queen Anne's Co; 30 December 1874; 27 May 1875

Johnson, Amos, 24, single, farm hand; Washington, Fannie J., 19, single, cook; 27 December 1883; 31 March 1884

Johnson, Charles, 21, single, laborer; Thompson, Ann Rebecca, 18, single; 25 January 1882; 28 January 1882

Johnson, Daniel, 25, single, farmhand; Phillett, Annie Amelia, 19, single, seamstress; 19 September 1878; 16 November 1878

Johnson, Eli, 21, single, laborer; Tillerson, Mary E., 16, single; 14 January 1880; 10 January 1880

Johnson, Essex Reed, 23, widower, farmhand; Wilson, Lizzie, 23, single, cook; 28 June 1883; 15 July 1884

Johnson, Frederick; Cooper, Henrietta, 24, single, servant; 8 December 1868; 2 January 1869

Johnson, George E., 24, single, farmhand; Wicker, Mary Matilda, 18, single, servant; 13 September 1877; 14 September 1877

Johnson, George W., 22, single, laborer; Freeman, Julia A., 21, single, cook; 1 December 1873; 24 July 1875

Johnson, George, 23, single, farmhand; Bowser, Augusta, 30, widow, servant; 8 October 1879; 29 November 1879

Johnson, Henry, 24, single, farmhand; Hynson, Lizzie, 22, single, servant; 8 September 1876; 19 September 1876

Johnson, Henry, 28, single, laborer; Hall, Louisa, 25, single, servant; 12 July 1868; 10 August 1868

Johnson, Henry, single; Green, Matilda; 13 January 1884; 8 February 1884

Johnson, Horace, 27, single, farmhand; Blake, Louisa, 21, single, housegirl; 14 September 1880; 15 September 1880

Johnson, Isaac, 46, widower, laborer; Crossley, Ann E., 21, single, servant; 20 May 1866; 7 February 1867

Johnson, James H., 20, single, laborer; Palmer, Clara, 16, single; 5 November 1868; 7 April 1869

Johnson, John W., 24, single, laborer; Brown, Sarah E., 22, single, cook; 25 December 1873; 31 December 1872

Johnson, John, 23, single, farmhand; Wright, Fanny, 21, single, servant; 27 December 1876; 3 February 1877

Johnson, John, 38, widower, farmhand; Johnson, Emma, 28, cook; 13 April 1882; 15 April 1882

Johnson, Joshua, 26, single, laborer; Lively, Nancy, single, servant; 19 June 1867; 26 October 1868

Johnson, Levin/Lewin, 24, widower, farmhand; White, Laura, 18, single, cook; 6 December 1883; 25 June 1884

Johnson, Lorenzo, 54, widower, fencer; Hines, Charlotte, 38, single, cook; 5 February 1885; 22 April 1885

Johnson, Moses, 22 single, farmhand; Woodland, Mary, 22, single, cook; 3 September 1880; 2 December 1880

Johnson, Perry, 22, single, fencer; White, Araminta, 18, House Girl, single; 17 May 1880; 1 July 1880

Johnson, Samuel, 21, single, laborer; Wallis, Anna, 17, single, servant; 19 November 1868; 16 January 1869

Johnson, Shade, 39, single, laborer; Thompson, Mary, 38, single, cook; 13 December 1877; 20 March 1877

Johnson, Thomas H., 22, single, farmhand; Smith, Henrietta, 17, single; 28 September 1877; 2 February 1877

Johnson, Thomas, 22, single, farmhand, Queen Anne's Co; Mitchell, Lucy, single; 29 April 1869; 7 October 1870

Johnson, Thomas, 29, single, servant; Doane, Jane, 18, single, servant; 28 December 1866; 3 January 1867

Johnson, William H; Cann, Amanda Ann, 16, single, servant; 15 September 1870; 3 March 1871

Johnson, William H., 26, single, farmhand; Reed, Augusta, 20, cook, single; 14 November 1882; 1 May 1883

Johnson, William H., 26, single, laborer; Graves, Elizabeth, 25, single, servant; 20 December 1868; 5 November 1868

Johnson, William H., 30, single, laborer; Johnson, Lotty Ann, 30, single, servant; 19 April 1868; 10 August 1868

Johnson, William Henry, 22 single, laborer; Riley, Mary M, 22, single, servant; 25 June 1868; 10 August 1868

Johnson, William Lee, 21, single, farmhand; Ringgold, Temperance C., 20, single, cook; 1 November 1882; 2 November 1882

Johnson, William W., 24, single, farmhand; Hamilton, Lucinda, 17, single, servant; 27 January 1876; 19 September 1876

Johnson, William, 55, laborer; Brown, Kitty, 50, single, cook; 8 June 1882; 17 June 1882

Jones Isaac G., 26, single, farmhand; Gleaves, Louisa, 18, single, cook; 24 July 1884; 31 July 1884

Jones, Andrew, 23, single, Hostler; Chambers, Hannah A., 22, single; 13 July 1885; 26 April 1886

Jones, Benjamin, 35, widower, farmhand; Brown, Ann Rebecca, 22, single, cook; 1 December 1881; 4 January 1882

Jones, Charles H., 23, single, laborer; Perkins, Fanny, 24, single, servant; 17 June 1868; 10 August 1868

Jones, Charles H., 24, single; Cole, Kate, 24, single; 5 November 1885; 5 November 1885

Jones, Charles, 27, single, laborer; Murray, Harriet, 27, servant, single; 21 June 1879; 22 June 1879

Jones, George W., 22, single, farmhand; Stewart, Angelina, 19, single, seamstress; 5 January 1882; 28 January 1882

Jones, Henry, 22, single, laborer; Phimoner, Kitty, 21, single, domestic; July 1876; 10 April 1876

Jones, Isaac, 32, single, laborer; Thomas, Eliza, 33, single, servant; 7 May 1868; 10 August 1868

Jones, James T., 32, single, laborer; Ringgold, Rachel A., 26, single, servant; 21 February 1870; 16 June 1870

Jones, John B., 22, single, barber; Comegys, Louisa, 22, single, servant; 18 July 1867; 9 August 1867

Jones, John H., 23, single, farmhand; Butler, Mary, 16, single, servant; 8 August 1877; 12 September 1877

Jones, John W., 29, single, farmhand; Kennard, Araminta, 24, single, cook; 30 October 1879; 22 April 1880

Jones, John Wesley, 25, single, farmhand; Johnson, Eliza, 24, single; 8 October 1874; 26 December 18767

Jones, John, 26, single, farmhand; Burden, Fanny, 20.5, single, servant; 25 May 1875; 10 August 1875

Jones, Junius, 28, single, farmhand; Goldsbourgh, Mary Ellen, 22, single, cook; 2 January 1879; 28 January 1879

Jones, Levi, 38, widower, carter; Frisby, Sarah Jane, 28, single; 12 January 1881 (Baltimore City); 21 January 1881

Jones, Louis, 21, single, laborer; Foreman, Caroline, 18, single, cook; 23 October 1873; 12 December 1872

Jones, Peter, 37, single, laborer; Frisby, Sallie, 29, widow, servant; 4 February 1869; 24 September 1869

Jones, Richard, 24, single, laborer; Nichols, Ella, 27, widow, cook; 3 June 1883; 12 June 1883

Jones, Samuel, 30, widower, farmhand; Thomas, Sophie, 24, single, servant; 17 April 1878; 31 August 1878

Jones, Thomas, 28, single, laborer; Posey, Eliza, 20, single, servant; 1866; 14 June 1867

Jones, William H., 26, single, laborer; Bowser Josephine, 16, single, servant; 16 January 1869

Jones,. Benjamin, 23, single, laborer; Butler, Ann Maria, 26, single, servant; 15 December 1870; 27 March 1871

Kane, Samuel, 50, widower, farmhand; Hynson, Martha, 25, single, cook; 21 July 1880; 27 July 1885

Kees, Buck, 25, single, farmhand; Banks, Lucy Ann, 19, single; 27 June 1886; 28 June 1886

Kelley, Alfred, 22, single, farmhand; Boyer, Eona, 20, single, cook; 6 March 1884; 8 March 1884

Kennard, Frederick, 32, single, farmhand; Raisin, Victoria, 24, single, servant; 9 November 1871; 8 March 1875

Kennard, Isaac H., 25, single, farmhand; Sages, Henrietta, 20, single, cook; 12 December 1883; 13 December 1883

Kennard, John E.; Starling, Mary A., 19; 27 December 1883; 19 January 1884

Kennard, Joseph H., 21, single, laborer; Tilghman, Mary, 20, single, servant; 25 November 1866; 14 May 1867

Kennard, Laurence, 26, single, laborer; Murray, Catherine, 26, single, cook; 11 October 1884; 14 October 1884

Kennard, Levi, 22, single, farmhand; Cammile, Mary E., 18, single, cook; 31 January 1863; 2 February 1883

Kennard, Samuel, 28, single, laborer; Tilghman, Mary, 18, single, servant; 26 September 1868; 16 January 1869

Kennard, Samuel, 55 10/12, widower, laborer; Sanders, Betsy, 57, widow, servant; 16 January 1869

Kennard, Thomas, 34, single, laborer; Welch, Louisa, 41, widow, laborer; 18 February 1873; 11 March 1873

Kennard, Wesley, 24, single, laborer; Jones, Sarah, 23, single, cook; 6 May 1873; 6 May 1873

Kesting, William T., 23, single, laborer; Freeman, Lizzie, 21, widow, servant; 21 December 1874; 16 August 1874

Key, William B., 39, single, laborer; Waters, Mary E., 26, single; 16 June 1880; 23 June 1880

Lambert, Henry, 23, single, laborer; Ballard, Sarah, 18, single, servant; 9 August 1866; 13 August 1866

Landsman, Henry, 25, single, laborer; Wright, Henrietta, 27, single, servant; 5 January 1871; 3 March 1871

Lansma, Alexander, 24, single, laborer; Leatherberry, Caroline, 24, widow, servant; 24 December 1868; 24 September 1869

Lee, Samuel, 22, single, laborer; Hutchins, Margaret, 20, single, cook; 26 September 1872; 4 October 1872

Lewis, Henry, 26, widower, farmer; Phillips, Laura, 21, single, nurse; 14 February 1884; 15 July 1884

Lewis, John, 40, widower, farmhand; Carroll, Hester, 18, single, cook; 2 November 1880; 2 December 1880

Lias, James H., 21, single, laborer; Graves, Amanda, 19, single, servant; 8 February 1869; 16 June1870

Liles, Charles, 21, single, Laborer; Moore, Harriet, 20, single; 20 November 1873; 25 June 1873

Liles, Fred, 36, single, laborer; Whale, Mary, 30, single, servant; 22 May ____; 18 February 1868

Liles, Frederick, 40, single, laborer; Purpose, Susan, 40, single, cook; 23 May 1872; 7 March 1872

Liles, James E., 25, single, farmhand; Jones, Mary C., 23, single, cook; 1 October 1885; 12 April 1886

Lindsay, Benjamin, 21, single, farmer; Houston, Ada, 30, single, cook; 18 October 1883; 12 February 1884

Lindsey, John Henry, 21, single, farmhand; Chatman, Mary Lizzie, 22, single, cook; 12 September 1881; 14 November 1881

Little, George, 28, widower, laborer; Moody, Mary E., 30, widow, cook; 12 October ____; 25 June 1873

Little, Joshua, 26, single, farmhand; Mason, Mary Ann, 23, single, cook; 25 October 1875; 14 December 1875

Little, Joshua, 60, widower, farmer; Johnson, Susan Ann, 50, widow; 6 November 1863; 18 November 1873

Lively, Isaiah, 19, single, laborer; Comegys, Mary R., 18, single, servant; 15 December 1869; 26 June 1870

Lively, Isaiah, 22, single, farmer; Woods, Harriet, 16, single, servant; 3 October 1871; 18 March 1872

Lively, Isaiah, 45, widower, farmer; Griffin, Sarah, 20, single, house girl; 26 June 1880; 2 December 1880

Lively, Levi, 23, single, farmhand; Colbert, Annie, 19, single, cook; 3 December 1882; 14 May 1883

Lockerman, Dave, 28, single, farmhand; Wheeders/Wheeler, Sadie, 29, widow, cook; 8 January 1885; 30 December 1885

Lockes, John, 53, widower, farmhand; Spencer, Emeline, 52, widow, washerwoman; 28 November 1877; 19 January 1880

Logan, John S., 22, single, laborer; Gleaves, Mary Ann, 18, single, servant; 15 June 1867; 12 July 1869

Maker, Lewis, 25, single, farmhand; Woodland, Jessie, 18, single, cook;
6 July 1886; 15 July 1886
Mander, Alexander, 23, farmer; Daniels, Letis, 18, cook; 9 September
1883; 4 May 1884
Mander, George, 24, single,. Laborer; Hunson, Mary, 18, single, servant;
26 January 1872; 15 July 1872
Mander, James, 37, widower, farmer; Hawkins, Henrietta, 43, widow,
cook; 7 February 1884; 19 February 1884
Mander, William, 23, single, laborer; Butcher, Sally, 20, single, servant;
1867; 14 June 1867
Martin, Alexander, 22, single, farmhand; Phillips, Jane, 19, single,
servant; 9 May 1877; 21 July 1871
Martin, Daniel W., 22, single, farmhand; Wilson, Clara, 20, single, cook;
4 January 1883; 9 January 1882
Martin, George Henry, 23, single, laborer; Milligan, Hester Ann, 22,
single, servant; 23 December 1869; 16 March 1870
Martin, Joseph, 27, single, laborer; Wilson, Mary J., 19, single, servant;
10 January 1867; 14 May 1867
Martin, Lewis, 22, single, farmhand; Wilson, Ann M., 18, cook; 18
December 1878; 4 January 1878
Martin, Perry, 23, single, sailor; Washington, Florence, 18, single, cook;
8 January 1885; 12 January 1885
Mason, Berry/Perry, 20, single, laborer; Chambers, Harriet, 18, single,
servant; 22 December 1868; 2 January 1869
Mason, Thomas, 21, single, laborer; Comegys, Mary, 18, single, servant;
8 November 1873
Mason, William H., 40, single, farmhand; Reed, Amanda Jane, 30,
single, cook; 9 August 1882; 9 December 1882
Massey, William H., 23, single, farmhand; Wicks, Mary L., 24, widow,
cook; 20 October 1879; 1 October 1879
Massey, William, 30, single, farmhand; Grooms, Margaret A., 35, single,
cook; 7 August 1884; 14 August 1884
Mather, Edward, 25, single, Laborer; Rasin, Sallie, 23, widow, servant;
19 September 1870; 16 March 1870
Matter, Elias, 29, single, farmhand; Riley, Catherine, 18, single, cook; 1
January 1885; 30 January 1885
Matter, John A., 25, single, farmhand; Wilmer, Dorothia, 29, single,
cook; 17 July 1881; 3 September 1881
Matthews, John H., 28, single, laborer; Caster/Casker, Henrietta, 28,
single, cook; 1 July 1886; 10 July 1886
Mattie, Elias, 21, widower, farmhand; Anderson, Julia, 19, single, cook;
5 June 1876; 1 September 1876

May, William H., 28, single, laborer; Gustus, Mary, 28, single, servant; 29 November 1869; 21 July 1871

Mays, Henry, 35, single, driver; Bowser, Anna, 30, single, cook; 10 July 1884; 21 February 1885

McCain, S. H., 37, single, laborer; Thompson, Henrietta, 26, single, servant; 26 October 1867; 18 February 1868

McCoy, Abraham, 31, single, barber; _alter, Mary C., 18, single, not employed; 18 March 1879; 19 March 1879

McDonald, Ira W., 27, single, laborer; Brown, Charlotte, 22, widow, servant; 10 January 1867; 24 April 1869

McQuery, Andrew. 22, single, farmhand; Brown, Mary C., 18, single, cook; 20 April 1886; 22 April 1886

Meeds, James W., 28, single, laborer; Mason, Mary J., 25, single; 27 December 1868

Miles, Francis, 28, single, farmhand; Starling, Mary, 38, single, cook; 2 January 1883; 4 June 1883

Miles, George W., 45, widower, farmer; Cooper, Lizzie, 35, single, cook; 17 March 1882; 14 May 1883

Miles, John, 25, single, laborer; Frisby, Debbie, servant; 22 May 1871; 16 June 1871

Miller, Aaron, 24, single, laborer; Butler, Martha, 16, single, servant; 26 February 1872; 25 June 1873

Miller, Aaron, 30, single, farmhand; Seeney, Julia, 26, single, cook; 6 January 1880; 22 April 1880

Miller, Charles, 27, single, farmhand; Scott, Mary L., 19, single, cook; 3 June 1880; 13 July 1880

Miller, Edward, 22, single, laborer; Roberts, Araminta, 22, single, servant; 26 November 1867; 25 June 1868

Miller, George, 25; Hyland, Delia, 21; 19 May 1872; 28 May 1872

Miller, Henry, 28, single, farmhand; Thomas, Augusta, 23, single, servant; 19 December 1877; 20 March 1877

Miller, Henry, 29, single, fisherman; Jackson, Teena, 29, widow, servant; 7-Apr-79; 9 April 1879

Miller, James, 35, widower, farmhand; Brown, Jane, 25, single, servant; 10 March 1881; 14 November 1881

Miller, James, 55, widower, laborer, Queen Anne's Co; Johnson, Henrietta, 51, widow, washerwoman; 6 March 1874; 9 March 1874

Miller, John H., 21, single, laborer; Gale, Anna E., 17, single, cook; 10 April 1871

Miller, Nelson, 55, widower, farmhand; Rasin, Margaret, 45, single, cook; 3 September 1885; 29 September 1885

Miller, Nelson, single; Riley, Araminta, single, cook; 5 June 1872; 6 June 1873

Milligan, George W., 35, widower, farmhand; Walley, Louisa, 30, single, cook; 12 October 1882; 5 December 1882

Millingan, George W., 22, laborer, single; Ford, Martha A, 19, single, servant; 9 April 1868

Mills, John William, 29, single, farmhand; Gleaves, Hester Ann, 35, widow, domestic; 29 July 1874; 1 August 1874

Mitchel, William H., 31, widower, farmhand; Wilmer, Georgetta, 27, widow, cook; 15 May 1884; 17 December 1884

Mitchell, George, 24, single, laborer; Johnson, Fannie, 16, single, cook; 14 April 1873; 12 December 1873

Mitchell, Henry A. W., 23, widower, farmhand; Turner, Nancy, 22, single, servant; 24 January 1877; 20 March 1877

Mitchell, John, 26, single, farmhand, Queen Anne's Co; Lawrence, Elizabeth, 28, single, cook, Queen Anne's Co; 13 January 1876; 23 October 1876

Mitchell, William, 25, single, farmhand; Blake, Mary Ann, 15, single, servant; 10 June 1876; 31 December 1876

Monroe, Charles H., 25, single, farmhand; Shields, Rachel, 21, single, cook; 17 May 1880; 19 May 1885

Morgan, James A., 22, single, farmhand; Doman, Rosa, 22, single, cook; 8 September 1880; 18 January 1881

Morris, Charles H., 34, widower, farmhand; Spencer, Araminta, 24, single, cook; 6 January 1885; 10 October 1885

Morris, William H., 24, single, farmhand; Spencer, Julia A., 20, single, servant; 27 October 1876; 30 October 1876

Morrison, William Reed, 23, single, laborer; Stewart, Harriett, 16, single, servant; 8 November 1873

Munson, John, 50, farmhand; Johnson, Charlotte, 38, servant; 27 February 1876; 14 March 1876

Murray, Abram, 27, single, laborer; Carter, Lucy, 26, widow, cook; 17 December 1884; 13 January 1885

Murray, James H., 24, single, laborer; Daniels, Cassy, 22, widow, servant; 19 September 1870; 16 March 1870

Murray, James, 32, single, laborer; Davis, Wilimina, 22, single, servant; 21 February 1876; 28 February 1876

Murray, John W., 26, single, laborer; Brown, Elizabeth, 19, single, not employed; 27 December 1877; 8 August 1878

Murray, Laurence, 30, single, driver, Queen Anne's Co; Laws, Mollie; 3 September 1885; 10 September 1885

Murray, William T., 36, single, laborer; Graves, Henrietta, 26, single, cook; 1 April 1880; 2 December 1881

Neal, James, 35, single, laborer; Comegys, Ann R., 20, single, servant; 23 March 1870; 16 June 1870

Neal, James, 35, single, laborer; Comegys, Ann R., 20, single, servant; 23 March 1870; 16 June 1870

Neal, Richard, 62, widower, waiter; Lee, Georgianna, 33, widow, cook; 6 January 1870; 6 June 1870

Neal, Richard, 62, widower, waiter; Lee, Georgeanna, 33, widow, cook; 6 January 1870; 16 June 1870

Nelson, Henry, 22, single, farmhand; Graves, Ella, 16, single, waiter (waitress); 30 December 1879; 1 January 1880

Newman, Henry, 24, single, laborer; Johnson, Charlotte, 22, single, cook; 17 September 1872; 21 September 1872

Newman, Henry, 24, single, laborer; Johnson, Charlot A., 22, single, cook; 17 September 1872; 21 September 1870

Newman, Henry, 25, widower, farmhand; Emory, Charlotte, 20, single, cook; 30 October 1879; 2 December 1879

Newton, James W., 47, widower, farmhand; Bordley, Rachel, 22, single; 26 October 1876; 14 June 1877

Nicholds, Frederick, 55, widower, farmhand; Bailey, Harriet, 35, widow, servant; 14 September 1876; 16 June 1877

Nichols, Frederick, 53, widower, farmhand; Bailey, Harriett, 35, widow, servant; 14 September 1876; 16 June 1876

Nichols, Frederick, 53, widower, laborer; Griffin, Harriett, 50, single, servant; 17 September 1868; 5 November 1868

Nichols, John Wesley, 28, single, groom; Pierce, Harret, 25, single, housekeeper; 3 April 1881; 14 November 1881

Nichols, Thomas, 26, single, farmhand; Pearce, Jane, 35, single, servant; 15 May 1875; 24 July 1875

Nichols, Thomas, 26, single, farmhand; Pearce, Jane, 35, single, servant; 15 May 1875; 24 July 1875

Nicholson, George, 64, widower, laborer; Redding, Annie, 58, widow, washerwoman; 4 November 1879; 26 November 1879

Nicholson, Jacob, 28, single, farmer; Robinson, Margaret, 20, single, servant; 10 January 1867; 9 August 1867

Norris, Isaac Henry, 29, single, farmhand; Wilson, Emma, 21, single, servant; 18 November 1876; 3 February 1877

Oliver, Henry, 50, widower, laborer; Riley, Susan, 50, widow, washerwoman; 14 June 1883; 15 June 1883

Page, Frederick, 26, single, farmhand; Wells, Amanda, 25, single, servant; 18 June 1874; 23 November 1874

Page, Joseph H., 21, single, laborer; Brown, Rachel, 24, single, cook; 19 October 1873; 24 July 1875

Parker, Andrew, 27, single, laborer; Hazzard, Mary Drusilla, 24, single, servant; 26 December 1871; 29 December 1871

Parker, Thomas, 24, single, farmhand; Davis, Carrie, 23, single, cook; 2 January 1883; 2 February 1883

Peaker, Levin, 25, single, farmhand; Wilson, Rosa, 18, single, cook; 12 January 1882; 16 May 1882

Pearce, James, 30, single, laborer; Glenn, Louisa, 27, single, servant; 10 March 1867; 11 November 1867

Pearce, John H., 45, single, farmhand; Jones, Ellen, 18, single, servant; 24 December 1876; 3 February 1877

Pearce, John, 22, single, farmhand; Butler, Annie, 19, single, servant; 13 June 1877; 21 July 1877

Pearce, Levin, 25, single, laborer; Chase, Catherine, 18, single; 14 May 1880; 15 May 1880

Pearce, Richard, 42, single, laborer; Glenn, Sarah C., 32, single, cook; 8 January 1880; 22 April 1880

Pearce, Thomas J., 23, single, farmhand; Tilghman, Rachel, 29, single; 2 September 1879; 21 August 1879

Peeker, Zachariah, 23, single, laborer; Sanders, Helen, 21, single, cook; 21 January 1869; 26 July 1869

Pennock, John F., 28; Harris, Caroline, 24; 14 January 1883; 5 June 1883

Perry, Alexander, single, farmhand; Phillips, Hester A., 19, single, cook; 3 July 1884; 21 July 1884

Perry, William Edward, 26, single, farmhand; Wallis, Mary Jane, 18 single, cook; 6 August 1882; 26 October 1882

Perry, William T., 23, single, laborer; Jenkins, Gracy A., 24, single; 11 July 1867; 24 April 1869

Philips, James Henry, 32, single, coachman; Thompson, Caroline, 70, widow, washerwoman; 7 February1877; 12 February 1877

Phillips, James W., 23, single, farmhand; Worrell, Hester V., 20, single, cook; 27 December 1883; 25 June 1884

Phillips, Thomas J., 34, single, farmhand; Stewart, Agnes, 37, widow, cook; 1 October 1884; 2 October 1884

Phillips, William A., 21 single, farmhand; Hynson, Annie E., 18, single; 19 January 1881; 3 February 1881

Phillips, William, 22, single, laborer; Ringgold, Sarah, 23, single, servant; 22 October 1868; 16 January 1869

Pierce, Eugene, 22, single, farmhand; Piner, Becky, 16, single, servant; 3 April 1881; 3 September 1881

Pierce, Miflin, 27, single, farmhand; Banks, Charlotte, 25, single, cook; 9 April 1885; 1 February 1888

Pierce, Richard, 22, single, farmhand; Brown, Caroline, 16, single, cook; 6 June 1881; 3 September 1881

Pierce, Thomas, 22, single, farmhand; Jones, Sarah Lizzie, 19, single, servant; 28 October 1875; 29 October 1875

Piner, Alexander, 24, single, farmhand; Barnes, Elizabeth, 30, single, servant; 23 September 1876; 28 October 1876

Piner, John, 45, widower, laborer; Hastings, Ellen, widow, cook; 23 December 1868; 25 June 1868

Pipes, Henry, 51, widower, farmer; Jeffers, Augusta, 39, widow, cook, Philadelphia, Pa; 3 March 1886; 16 March 1886

Pipes, Samuel George, 24; Roe, Julia, 18, single, cook; 17 January 1884; 4 April 1884

Poindexter, Jacob, 44, single, laborer; Johnson, Hester, 52, single, cook; 12 May 1881; 14 May 1881

Porter, Edward, 23, single, laborer; Chase, Louisa, 18, single, servant; 25 April 1868; 7 August 1872

Porter, Henry, 22, single, laborer; Rigby, Elizabeth, 17, single, cook; 5 March 1884; 31 March 1884

Porter, John, 23, single, farmer; Tilghman, Julia J., 19, single; 12 November 1885; 24 November 1885

Pratt, Abraham, 23, single, laborer; Johnson, Milcah, 20, single, servant; 26 December 1866; 9 August 1867

Pratt, Joseph, 22, single, farmhand; Beverly, Mary, 18, single, cook; 21 December 1882; 16 March 1883

Preston, Henry, 21, single, laborer; Demby, Charlotte, 22, single, servant; 6 October 1871; 28 December 1871

Price, E. L., 37, widower, Engineer, Philadelphia, Pa; Brown, Maria, 37, single, cook; 25 September 1883; 8 January 1884

Price, Edward, 38, single, laborer; Brown, Harriet, 19, single, cook; 21 April 1885; 12 April 1886

Price, Joseph, 23, single, farmhand; Saunders, Jane, 19, single, cook; 8 May 1884; 17 May 1884

Price, Oliver, 23, single, farmer; Chambers, Mary E., 26, single, cook; 2 November 1871; 6 November 1870

Raisin, George W. Sr., 46, single, farmhand; White, Mary A., 20, single, cook; 10 May 1882; 5 December 1882

Raisin, Richard, 19, single, farmhand; Smallwood, Clara, 20, single, not employed; 10 August 1876; 3 February 1877

Raisin, Samuel, 23, single, farmhand; Miller, Ann M., 40, widow, cook; 24 December 1878; 4 April 1879

Rasin, Arthur, 23, single, laborer; Hackett, Victoria, 19, single, servant; 7 April 1874; 28 April 1874

Rasin, Isaiah, 22, single, farmhand; Freeman, Annie, 17, single, cook; 15 March 1885; 28 April 1885

Rasin, Ishmaiul, 23, single; Spencer, Annie J., 17; 23 July 1883; 4 October 1883

Rasin, James Laws, 40, widower, laborer; Price, Caroline, 34, widow, cook; 20 June 1866; 3 July 1866

Rasin, James, 48, widower, farmhand; Young, Amanda, 28, widow, cook; 15 March 1883

Rasin, John, 21, single, farmhand; Perry, Rebecca, 18, single, servant; 30 December 1876; 21 August 1877

Rasin, Moses, 41, widower, cook; Jones, Rachel, 40, widow, cook; 17 August 1884; 15 November 1884

Rasin, Warner, 38, widower, farmhand; Rasin, Laura, 26, single, cook; 4 January 1883; 15 January 1889

Rasin, William, 36, single, laborer; Thomas, Amanda, 21, single, cook; 27 January 1870; 6 May 1870

Rasin, Louis, 28, single, farmhand; Tilghman, Henrietta, 23, single, cook; 18 April 1881; 23 April 1881

Reading, William T, 50, widower, farmhand; Wickes, Mary J., 50, single, cook; 9 January 1883; 9 May 1883

Redding, Alexander, 22, single, coachman; Jones, Linda, 18, single, waitress; 12 September 1883; 31 March 1884

Redding, Benjamin, 23, single, farmhand; Derry, Mary E., 22, single, cook; 12 August 1884; 15 November 1884

Redding, John, 40, single, farmhand; Tilghman, Alphonsa, 20, single, cook; 17 January 1878; 8 February 1879

Reed, Abraham, 21, single, laborer; Chambers, Martha, 15, single, servant; 18 November 1868; 16 January 1869

Reed, Nelson, 45, single, carter; Miller, Rachel, 40, widow; 21 December 1882; 18 June 1883

Reed, Noah J., 22, single, farmhand; Hynson, Ella, 23, single, cook; 23 June 1881; 18 July 1881

Reed, Prince, 30 single, farmhand; Dorsey, Olivia, 17, single, servant; 19 December 1876; 3 February 1877

Rees, Charles H., 24, single, sailor; Sheppard, Annie, 25, single, house girl; 13 September 1882; 14 May 1883

Reese, Adolphus, 23, single, hostler; Anderson, Catherine, 18, single, cook; 4 December 1884; 9 November 1885

Reese, Jeremiah, 24, single, farmhand; Bailey, Mary Jane, 25, widow, cook; 16 August 1879; 16 August 1879

Reese, Joseph, 21, single, farmhand; Hales, Louisa, 22, single, servant; 13 March 1878; 15 March 1878

Reese, William Thomas, 25, single, farmhand; Warner, Anna Maria, 24, single, cook; 17 August 1875; 18 August 1875

Richardson, Benjamin, 28, single, laborer; Lee, Sarah M., 25, single, cook; 13 December 1870; 21 March 1871

Richardson, John, 24, single, laborer; Griffin, Georgeanna, 24, single, cook; 18 September 1871; 5 September 1871

Richardson, Joseph, 23, single, laborer; Anderson, Annie, 18, single, servant; 26 July 1868; 29 September 1868

Richardson, William H., 24, single, laborer; Tilghman, Caroline, 26, single, servant; 26 March 1871; 27 March 1871

Riding, James, 21, single, farmhand; Goldsborough, Martha, 19, single, cook; 31 March 1880; 1 April 1880

Rigby, Henry, 22, single, laborer; Barroll, Sarah R., 17, single, servant; 11 August 1868; 2 January 1869

Riley, E., 49, widower, laborer; Wilson, Susan, 25, widow, servant; 28 May 1874; 29 May 1874

Riley, Francis, 24, single, farmhand; Scott, Elizabeth, 22, single; September 1880; 4 April 1884

Riley, Frederick, 55, widower, farmhand; Myers, Annie, 52, cook; 8 April 1882; 11 April 1882

Riley, George W., 24, single; Driver, Amy, 22, single; 8 January 1885; 10 January 1885

Riley, James H., 22, single, laborer; Urie, Emeline, 22, single, cook; 17 October 1870; 3 March 1871

Riley, Samuel, 24, single, farmhand; Foreman, Mary E., 25, single, cook; 5 June 1879; 11 June 1879

Riley, Thomas, 23, single, laborer; Jones, Harriet, 20, single, servant; 29 December 1869; 16 June 1870

Riley, Thomas, 26, single, farmhand; Wilson, Harriet, 30, single, cook; 4 January 1884; 15 July 1884

Riley, Wesley, 28, single, laborer; Reed, Debby, 28, single, servant; 13 October 1869; 16 June 1870

Riley, William E., 25, single, laborer; Ward, Susan Jane, 20, single, domestic; 26 October 1874; 23 November 1874

Riley, William Edward, 22, single, laborer; Butler, Henrietta, 21, single, servant; 25 August 1870; 19 September 1870

Riley, William, 25, single, laborer; Blake, Ellen, 18, single, servant; 1866; 14 June 1867

Riley, William, 45, single, laborer; Boyer, Susan, 35, single, cook; 12 November 1873; 12 December 1873

Ringgold, Charles H., 21, single, farmhand; Berryman, Maria, 19, single, cook; 9 December 1880; 18 December 1880

Ringgold, Elijah, 26, single, farmhand; Brown, Kate, 26, single, cook; 15 January 1878; 13 May 1878

Ringgold, George W., 25, single, farmhand; Kennard, Martha, 25, single, not employed; 29 October 1879; 8 November 1879

Ringgold, George, 46, widower, laborer; Hynson, Caroline, widow, cook; 18 March 1872; 18 March 1872

Ringgold, Henry, 21, single, laborer; Broadway, Mary E., 16, single, servant; 5 April 1866; 13 November 1866

Ringgold, John Henry, 21, single, farmhand; Doman, Lizzie, 19, single, house girl; 6 June 1880; 13 July 1880

Ringgold, John W., 23, single, laborer; Trusty, Henrietta, 19, single, cook; 8 October 1871; 25 June 1873

Ringgold, John, 40, widower, farmhand; Ennis, Annie, 35, single, cook; 30 December 1884; 10 January 1885

Ringgold, Levi, 25, single, laborer; Thompson, Mary J., 21, single, cook; 25 August 1866; 14 May 1867

Ringgold, Levi, 25, single, laborer; Ewing, Elizabeth, 20, single, cook; 5 January 1873; 25 June 1873

Ringgold, Levi, 28, single, laborer; Rasisn, Jane Louisa, 23, single, servant; 24 October 1872; 25 June 1873

Ringgold, Lewis, 25, single, farmhand; Lindsey, Mary, 18, single; 23 November 1883; 15 July 1884

Ringgold, Robert, 21, single, laborer; Anderson, S., J., 25, single, servant; 1873; 12 December 1873

Ringgold, Robert, 25, widower, farmhand; Brown, Harriet, 26, widow, servant; 12 September 1876; 12 September 1876

Ringgold, Simon, 22, single, farmhand; Irving, Mary Francis, 22, single, cook; 5 January 1882; 17 January 1882

Ringgold, William, 21, single, laborer; Barroll, Sarah E., 18, single, cook; June 1869; 22 December 1869

Robbins, Gilbert H., 28, single, farmhand; Cooper, Maria Louisa, 29, widow, not employed; 4 December 1879; 19 January 1880

Roberts, Isaac, 29, single, laborer; Anderson, Margaret, 21, single, cook; 13 December 1870; 27 March 1871

Roberts, James, 26, single, laborer; Chambers, Elizabeth, 25, single, servant; 16 November 1867; 25 June 1868

Robinson, Henry T., 25, single, farmhand; Brice, Maggie, 19, single, cook; 27 October 1881; 25 March 1882

Robinson, John David, 23, single, farmhand; Hynson, Ellen, 18, single, cook; 27 May 1879; 22 April 1880

Robinson, John, 27, single, laborer; Johnson, Adeline, 29, widow, cook; 24 April 1873; 3 May 1873

Rochester, James H., 44, widower, farmer; Hodges, Ellen, 24, single, cook; 11 January 1880; 13 January 1880

Roe, John, 33; Single, Annie, 21; 4 October 1885; 12 October 1885

Rogers, James E., 29, single, janitor; Chase, Maria, 26, single, cook; 17 July 1879; 22 July 1879

Rogers, Levi, 51, widower, carter; Brooks, Milly, 50, widow, fameress; 7 December 1865; 18 February 1866

Rogester, William H., 55, single, farmhand; Gibbs, Emily, 40, widow, cook; 17 April 1884; 18 April 1884

Rose, James, 35, single, farmhand; Davis, Charlotte, 33, widow, cook; 15 January 1880; 21 January 1880

Royal, Daniel A., 24, single; Smith, Mary A., 22, single, cook; 26 December 1877; 22 April 1880

Russell, John F., 25, single, farmhand; Mason, Alberta, 18, single, cook; 4 August 1885; 25 April 1885

Russum, William D., 28, single, laborer; Seney, Martha Jane, 18, single, cook; 7 March 1873; 15 March 1873

Sampson, Edward, 25, single, farmhand; Garrison, M. Laura, 16, single, not employed; 26 May 1880; 7 August 1880

Sampson, Isaac, 29, widower, farmer; Stewart, Catherine, 20, single, servant; 12 January 1876; 21 August 1877

Sampson, Joseph, 31, single, laborer; Boyer, Sarah, 21, single; 28 April 1872; 25 June 1873

Sampson, Joseph, 31, single, laborer; Boyer, Sarah I., 21, single, cook; 28 April 1872; 25 June 1873

Sampson, Samuel, 23, single, laborer; Wing, Anna Maria, 23, single, servant; 1866; 5 June 1867

Sanders, Harrison, 27, single, laborer; Brice, Henrietta, 30, single, servant; 29 December 1868; 9 January 1869

Sanders, James E., 24, single, farmhand; Hall, Laura, 21, single, servant; 14 September 1877; 12 August 1877

Savage, George, 21, single, farmhand; Seney, Irene, 24, single, cook; 6 November 1883; 25 June 1884

Saxon, Isaac, 33, single, laborer; Johns, Annie, 25, single, cook; 20 October 1881; 29 November 1881

Scott, Albert L., 42, single, farmhand; Tillison, Annie, 39, single, cook; 22 November 1877; 28 November 1877

Scott, Henry, 25, single, fisherman; White, Maria, 23, single, cook; 30 April 1880; 7 May 1880

Scott, James H., 21, single, farmhand; Comegys, Hannah, 19, single, cook; 26 December 1883; 2 January 1884

Scott, James Wesley, 23, single, farmhand; Wilmer, Laura L., 14, single, servant; 1879; 10 January 1879

Scott, James, 23, single, workman; Gleeves, Annie, 21, single, cook; 26 December 1878; 24 De3cember 1878

Scott, Joseph, 37, single, farmhand; Castle, Marie, 35, single, cook; 26 June 1881; 7 July 1882

Scott, Josiah, 24; Hall, Mary L., 20; 25 May 1884; 15 August 1884

Scott, Samuel, 24, single, laborer; Thomas, Rachel, 16, single, servant; 27 May 1871; 7 August 1871

Scott, Samuel, 35, single, laborer; Brown, Anna Eliza, 29, single, servant; 1867; 14 June 1867

Scott, Samuel, 45, widower, farmhand; Fogwell, Ann E., 45, single, cook; 18 September 1879; 27 October 1879

Seigle, Paul, 24, widower, farmhand; Woodland, Jane, 24, widow, servant; 31 December 1876; 10 April 1876

Seney, Charles A., 25, single, farmhand; Lamden, Susie Clara, 16, single, house girl; 16 August 1881; 17 August 1881

Seney, William H., 24, single, farmhand; Scott, Addie, 19, single, house girl; 25 May 1885; 26 May 1885

Sewell, James A., 21, single, farmhand; Brown, Mary M., 19, single, cook; 16 November 1882; 5 December 1882

Sheppard, Henry, 20, single, farmhand; Ford, Annie, 22, single, cook; 3 November 1880; 21 February 1881

Sheppard, John Wesley, 22, single, laborer; Deaker, Mary Ellen, 20, single, servant; 12 June 1879; 16 September 1879

Signers, Paul, 24, single, laborer; Graves, Louisa, 18, single, cook; 2 September 1871; 25 June 1873

Simmonds, George, 26, single, waiter; Ward, Anna, 18, single, seamstress; 16 June 1870; 21 July 1871

Simmonds, William H., 23, single, laborer; Brown, Gulilluia, 17, single, none; 26 July 1873; 24 July 1874

Simmons, John H., 29, single, farmhand; White, Hariet M., 17, single; 30 October 1883; 25 June 1884

Simon, Chas_ A., 23, sailor, single; Reed, Emma, 23, single, dressmaker; 15 June 1881; 14 November 1881

Sindell, Thomas H., 22, single, farmhand; Freeman, Jane, 21, single, servant; 26 August 1876; 28 October 1876

Singer, Richard I., 27, single, farmhand; Davis, Laura, 20, single, house girl; 31 August 1881; 25 February 1881

Sisco, Thomas, 21, single, farmhand; Johnson, Laura, 18, single, cook; 11 November 1882; 18 November 1882

Sisngleton, Josiah, 27, single, farmhand; Shields, Annie M., 28, single, servant; 13 December 1876; 20 March 1877

Slaughter, Charles H., 40, single, laborer; Willis, Ann, 40, widow, servant; 30 December 1872; 3 May 1873

Smallwood, Anthony, 25, single, laborer; Murray, Mary, 18, single, servant; 12 August 1866; 5 June 1867

Smallwood, Anthony, 35, widower, farmhand; Jones, Jane, 35, single; 16 August 1881; 22 August 1881

Smallwood, Archie, 22, single, laborer; Goseling, Aliza, 19, single, chambermaid; 16 April 1870; 27 September 1870

Smallwood, Samuel, 25, single, laborer; Thompson, Rachel, 39, single, cook; 8 January 1873; 25 June 1873

Smallwood, Thomas, 24, single, laborer; Graves, Anna M., 22, single, washerwoman; 11 December 1868; 2 January 1869

Smallwood, William, 24, single, farmhand; Brown, Marietta, 18, single, servant; 31 December 1876; 10 April 1876

Smith, Archer, 26, single, waiter; Wright, Henrietta, 28, widow, servant; 25 October 1876; 2 October 1876

Smith, Edward Hynson, 49, single, farmhand; Thomas, Ann Rebecca, 49, widow, cook; 28 November 1877; 28 December 1877

Smith, George Alfred, 28, single, laborer; Bell, Susan, 20, single, house girl; 21 March 1880; 2 December 1880

Smith, George H., 21, single, laborer; Kelly, Sarah G., 22, single, cook; 28 January 1869; 30 January 1869

Smith, Hynson, 30, single, farmhand; Miller, Octavia, 29, single, cook; 12 September 1883; 14 May 1883

Smith, Isaac; Toomy, Catherine; 7 April 1869

Smith, James Henry, 22, single, farmhand; Green, Marissa, 17, single, cook; 22 October 1885; 28 October 1885

Smith, Jeremiah, 28 3/12, single, laborer; Chambers, Elizabeth, 23, single, servant; 28 June 1868; 1 April 1869

Smith, John, 28, single, farmhand; Riley, Martha D., 25, single, cook; 23 November 1884; 3 December 1884

Smith, John, 40, widower, farmhand; Miller, Sarah Maria, 15, single, cook; 29 December 1879; 5 January 1800

Smith, John, 45, single, farmhand; Brookins, Louisa, 25, single, cook; 19 December 1878; 22 April 1880

Smith, Simon, 25, single, laborer; Thompson, Ginger (?), 17, single, servant; 21 September 1867; 1 October 1867

Smith, Simon, 36, widower, farmer; Brookins, Lizzie, 26, single, housekeeper; 4 January 1880; 6 January 1880

Smith, Solomon, 28, single, laborer; Ward, Augustus, 19, single, cook; 30 December 1883; 15 July 1884

Smith, Thomas, 21, single, laborer; Snowden, Eliza, 45, widow; 27 June 1874; 16 March 1883

Smith, William Henry, 51, widower, hostler; Tilghman, Susan, 45, widow, domestic; 21 November 1874; 24 July 1875

Smyth, John Henry, 24, single, farmhand; Wright, Ella, 18, single, seamstress; 10 April 1880; 16 April 1880

Snowden, Joseph, 21, single, farmhand; Jones, Eliza A., 19, single, cook; 24 April 1884; 13 May 1884

Sorrell, Robert, 23, single, farmhand; Redding, Ann E., 24, widow, servant; 31 December 1878; 4 January 1879

Spencer, Frisby, 25, single, farmhand; Wilson, Susan, 26, single, cook; 6 December 1884; 18 December 1884

Spencer, William Henry, 21, single, farmhand; Miller, Martha Jane, 20, single, cook; 26 November 1885; 28 November 1885

Stanley, Samuel I., 26, single, laborer; Butler, Ann E. C., 18, single, servant; March 1873; 12 December 1873

Stephens, Charles H., 30, single, farmhand; Smallwood, Martha, 30, single, cook; 12 October 1882; 26 October 1882

Stephenson, Samuel, 22, single, farmer; Anderson, Adeline, 19, single, servant; 26 August 1869; 7 July 1870

Stevens, John, 26, single, laborer; Dixon, Mary E., single, servant; 15 July 1873; 6 May 1884

Stevenson, John, 36, widower, farmhand; Berry, Sylvia Ann, 34, widow, none; 17 March 1876; 2 October 1876

Stewart, Alexander, 45, single, farmhand; Worrell, Charlotte, 40, single, house woman; 14 August 1883; 15 July 1884

Stewart, Philip, 20 single, laborer; Thomas, Anna, 18, single, cook; February 1874; 1 August 1876

Stewart, Thomas H., 24, single, farmhand, Baltimore County; Wilmor, Laura J., 17, single, housework; 3 November 1880; 4 November 1880

Stewart, Thomas, 27, single, laborer; Walker, Annie R., 19, single, cook; 31 June 1885; 4 January 1886

Stockley, William Henry, 50, single, farmhand; Riley, Eliza, 50, single, servant; 18 June 1876; 10 April 1876

Stouts, Joshua T., 23, single, farmhand; Jones, Georganna, 18, single, house girl; 23 March 182; 16 May 1882

Strickering, John L., 24, single, laborer; Anderson, Rebecca, 23, single, servant; 28 December 1873; 6 June 1873

Strickning, Elijah, 27, single, waiter; Smith, Isabel, 25, single, servant; 4 August 1880; 7 August 1880

Strong, Richard, 45, single, farmer; Johnson, Carrie, 25, single, cook; 31 January 1884; 2 February 1884

Stuart, George W., 22, single, farmhand; Thomas, Martha J., 20, single, cook; 18 January 1883; 9 May 1883

Stuart, Jacob, 35, widower, farmhand; Gooling, Jane, 32, single, cook; 8 January 1871; 21 July 1871

Stuart, Thomas, 24, widower, farmhand; Starling, Annie, 23, single, cook; 16 January 1883; 9 May 1883

Sudler, Solomon, 23, single, farmhand; Thomas, Ella, 18, single, servant; 1 February 1877; 7 February 1877

Suskey, George Thomas, 25, single, laborer; Warner, Katie, 17, single; 4
February 1883; 6 February 1883
Suskey, George Thomas, 25, single, laborer; Warner, Katie, 17, single; 4
February 1883; 6 February 1883
Sutton, Samuel, 45, farmhand, Cecil Co; Dapson, Eliza, 41, house
servant, Cecil Co; 21 January 1869; 26 July 1869
Swift, Jacob Henry, 41, widower, farmhand; Anderson, Margaret, 39,
single, cook; 28 June 1883; 15 July 1884
Syiller, Frisby Gordon, 31, single, farmhand; Graves, Lizzie, 18, single,
cook; 6 August 1885; 12 April 1886
Tanner, Lewis, 60, widower, laborer; Williams, Eliza, 60, widow, cook;
13 September 1872; 17 September 18172
Tanner, Louis, 24, single, laborer; Frisby, Salina, 16, single; 15
September 1868; 19 September 1868
Taylor, Edward, 35, single, farmhand; Brown, Priscilla, 40, widow, cook;
31 August 1880; 25 February 1881
Taylor, Henry, 22, single, sailor; Thomas, Louisa, 18, single, cook; 14
October 1884; 17 December 1884
Taylor, Turner, 25, single, farmhand; Hazzard, Emma, 23, single, cook;
16 December 1871; 20 December 1871
Taylor, Warren, 20, single, laborer; Caulk, Mintie (Araminta?), 18,
single, cook; 10 January 1884; 8 February 1884
Taylor, Zachariah, 21, single, laborer; Hall, Kitty, 23, single, servant; 18
March 1869; 24 September 1869
Tench, James A., 21, single, laborer; Pearce, Laura, 24, single, servant;
19 August 1869; 24 September 1869
Tench, William, 46, widower, laborer; Spencer, Elizabeth, 26, single,
servant; 24 October 1867; 14 March 1868
Thomas, B. W., 21, single, laborer; Chaney, Anna M., 20, single, cook;
18 February 1870; 16 June 1870
Thomas, Charles Henry, 21, single, farmhand; Barrett, Mamie, 21,
single, housegirl; 1 June 1882; 3 June 1882
Thomas, Edward, 27, single, laborer; Thompson, Elizabeth, 26, single,
servant; 19 December 1867; 14 March 1868
Thomas, Horace, 54, widower, farmhand; Goldsborough, Caroline, 60,
widow, cook; 12 April 1883; 1 May 1883
Thomas, James H., 24, single, farmhand; Carter, Louisa, 20, single, cook;
20 September 1883; 22 December 1883
Thomas, James, 29, single, farmhand; Ringgold, Rachel, 25, single,
cook; 23 December 1882; 23 December 1882
Thomas, James, 33, single, farmhand; Toulson, Harriet Ann, 19, single,
servant; 17 October 1878; 28 October 1876

Thomas, John H., 26, single, coachman; Johnson, Elizabeth, 24, single, servant; 8 February 1877; 12 February 1877

Thomas, John, 22, single, laborer; Gant, Tilly, 24, single, cook; 29 March 1880; 21 April 1880

Thomas, John, 42, single, laborer; Gaddis, Laura, 32, single, cook; 3 April 1883; 13 April 1883

Thomas, Joseph, 21, single, farmhand; Harrison, Annie, 20, single, cook; 25 April 1878; 22 May 1878

Thomas, Wesley, 24, widower, farmhand; Bowser, Martha, 35, widow, cook; 23 June 1885; 14 December 1885

Thomas, William, 25, single, farmhand; Wilmer, Mary Jand, 16, single, servant; 7 January 1879; 22 January 1879

Thomas, William. H., 22, single, laborer, Queen Anne's Co; Demby, George Ann, 18, single, house woman, Queen Anne'; 19 August 1872; 22 August 1872

Thomas. John H., 31, single, farmhand; Porter, Henrietta, 24, single, cook; 3 July 1884; 15 July 1884

Thompson (?), Philip H., 34, single, tailor; Murrey (?), Sarah Ann, 26, single, domestic; 28 August 1871; 24 September 1871

Thompson, Benjamin, 27, single, farmhand; Hastings, Ann Rebecca, 16, single, house girl; 2 August 1883; 25 June 184

Thompson, Frank, 37, widower, farmhand; Hazel, Arabella, 29, widow, hair dresser, Philadelphia, Pa; 15 October 1864; 24 October 1884

Thompson, George A., 28, single, farmhand; Johnson, Harriet E., 16, single, cook; 30 July 1881; 1 October 1881

Thompson, Henry, 35, single, farmhand; Craig, Elizabeth, 20, single, cook; 24 January 1884; 2 February 1884

Thompson, James W., 23, single, laborer; Moore, Mary I., 18, single, servant; 8 November 1873

Thompson, John E., 20, single, farmhand; Jones, Alice J.,18, single, servant; 6 July 1876; 5 September 1876

Thompson, John, 27, single, laborer; Wilson, Martha, 26, single, cook; 11 May 1882; 13 May 1884

Thompson, Jonah, 24, single, farmhand; Thomas, Mary C., 21, single, servant; 5 June 1876; 5 September 1876

Thompson, Joshua, 25, single, farmhand; Graves, Rebecca, 18, single, cook; 12 May 1885; 19 May 1885

Thompson, Samuel H., 25, single, laborer; Turner, L. I., 15, single, servant; 9 January 1873; 6 June 1873

Thompson, Samuel, 21, single, laborer; Wickes, Sallie, 17, single, servant; 25 March 1869; 12 July 1869

Thompson, Samuel, 45, widower, farmhand; Gibbs, Rebecca, 35, widow, servant; 28 December 1876; 10 April 1876

Thompson, Samuel, 80, widower, farmhand; Dunbar, Ann Rececca; 19 February 1880; 10 March 1880

Thompson, Thomas, 30, single, farmhand; Handy, Georgianna, 25, single, cook; 8 April 1876; 5 September 1876

Thompson, William H., 21, single, farmhand; Rasin, Sarah, M., 18, single, cook; 10 March 1881; 4 March 1881

Tilghman, Alexander, 35, single, farmhand; Tilghman, Edith, 25, single, cook; 4 July 1881; 2 August 1881

Tilghman, Alfred M., 27, widower, laborer; Harrison, Editha, 17, single, servant; 25 September 1874

Tilghman, Ebenezer, 24, single, laborer; Wilson, Ellen, widow, cook; 14 May 1870; 21 July 1871

Tilghman, John W., 22, single, laborer; Beauchamp, Glacy E., 23, single, servant; 7 June 1867; 9 August 1867

Tilghman, John W., 25, single, laborer; Houston, Hannah E., 16, single, servant; 25 December 1873; 21 December 1873

Tilghman, John, 32, widower, farmhand; Cotton, Tempe A., 18, single, cook; 16 November 1881; 14 March 1882

Tilghman, Levi B., 24, single, laborer; Ross, Sarah E. L., 17, single, servant; 12 October 1880; 21 February 1881

Tilghman, Levi, 30, single, laborer; Cain, M. Elizabeth.,21, single, cook; 15 September 1870; 3 March 1871

Tilghman, Theodore, 33, widower, farmhand; Ringgold, Augustus, 20, single, cook; 18 November 1883; 15 November 1884

Tilghman, William H., 21, single, farmhand; Graves, Margaret, 21, single, cook; 7 February 1883; 9 February 1883

Tilghman, William Henry, 21, single, farmhand; Bentley, Henrietta, 19, single, servant; 18 September 1878; 9 September 1878

Tilghman, Daniel Columbus, 21, single, farmhand; Banks, Lottie, 16, single, cook; 2 September 1877; 18 September 1877

Tiller, George, 23, single, farmhand; Dorsey, Eliza, 18, single, servant; 25 November 1876; 27 November 1876

Tiller, Joseph James, 89, widower, laborer; Willson, Mary, 23, single, cook; 8 January 1880; 17 January 1880

Tillison, Eben, 43, single, farmhand; Woodland, Julia, 19, single, cook; 31 December 1881; 3 January 1882

Tillison, Samuel, 22, single, farmhand; Harris, Mary Agnes, 17, single, cook; 2 January 1878; 26 January 1878

Titter, Maney, 23, single, farmhand; Harding, Alice, 23, single, servant; 13 December 1874; 27 May 1875

Toulson, Stephen, 28, single, laborer; Segg, Mary, 25, single, cook; 7 January 1869; 17 February 1869

Towson, Alexander, 21, single, farmhand; Johnson, Annie M., 19, single; 24 August 1881; 1 October 1881

Trusty, John W. H., 25, single, farmhand; Brown, Henrietta, 18, single; 28 December 1870; 21 July 1871

Trusty, Joseph, 29, single, farmhand; Kilson, H. E. M., 22, single, cook; 13 January 1881; 1 January 1860

Trusty, Perre, 22, single, laborer; Blake, Henrietta, 16, single, cook; March 1873; 12 December 1873

Tubman, Joseph, 23, single, farmhand; Segar, Jane, 20, single, cook; 5 October 1880; 21 February 1881

Turner, Francis A., 32, widower, farmhand; Griffith, Sarah, 16, single, domestic; 31 March 1874; 4 June 1880

Turner, Frederick, 24, single, laborer; Tilghman, Emily Elizabeth, 18, single, house servant; 15 March 1866; 13 August 1866

Turner, George W., 23, single, laborer; Kirby, Annie E., 19, single; 15 October 1873; 23 November 1873

Tyler, John, 34, single, fisherman; Dickenson, Cora, 20, single, servant; 2 June 1886; 3 July 1886

Wadkins, Albert, 25, single, laborer; Bradshaw, Adeline, 22, single, cook; 12 September 1867; 14 March 1868

Walker, John, 25, single, laborer; Hynson, Geo Anna (Georgeanna?), 19, single, cook; 23 October 1873; 12 December 1873

Walley, James O., 21, single, farmhand; Chambers, Frances M., 21, single, cook; 6 February 1879; 8 February 1879

Walley, Perry, 26, single, farmhand; White, Catherine, 23, single, cook; 1 June 1875; 10 August 1875

Walley, Richard, 26, widower, laborer; Beown, Harriett, 21, single, cook; 3 December 1874; 24 July 1875

Wallis, Daniel, 23, single, farmhand; Green, Mary, 22, single, cook, Baltimore City; 22 January 1884; 31 March 1884

Wallis, John, 27, single, farmhand; Anderson, Evalina, 16, single, servant; 7 January 1879; 8 February 1879

Wally, Adam, 33, single, farmhand; Mcgraith, Amanda, 30, single, cook; 8 August 1885; 8 August 1885

Wally, Alexander, 24, single, farmhand; Brown, Elizabeth, 21, single, cook; 25 September 1884; 7 October 1884

Wally, Frederick, 35, widower, farmhand; Carroll, Sarah, 25, widow, cook; 30 October 1884; 1 November 1884

Wally, John, 22, single, farmhand; Doman, Annie, 28, single, servant; 5 January 1876; 10 April 1876

Wally, Richard, 25, single, laborer; Scott, Sarah, 30, single, cook; 28 December 1882; 15 July 1884

Ward, Albert, 21, single, farmhand; Morgan, Jennie, 18, single, cook; 29 December 1885; 9 January 1885

Ward, Emory, 21, single, farmhand; Jones, Ellen, 17, single, domestic; 12 March 1874; 1 August 1876

Ward, Jefferson; Wright, Eliza; 26 October 1867; 18 February 1867

Ward, Lewis H., 26, single, farmhand; Berryman, Lucy, 17, single, cook; 25 February 1886; 26 February 1886

Ward, P. H. D., 32, single, servant; Salter, Caroline, 22, single; 17 October 1876; 14 June 1877

Ward, Richard T., 32, single, farmer; Hamilton, Mary R., 19, single, seamstress; 4 October 1878; 22 April 18880

Ward, Richard, 28, single, laborer; Leias, Alice, 18; 19 August 1868; 16 January 1869

Ward, Richard, 41, widower, laborer; Blackistone, Sarah, 35, widow, cook; 27 May 1886; 1 June 1885

Ward, William, 24, single, farmhand; Lively, Adeline, 20, single, servant; 21 December 1876; 21 July 1877

Warner, George W., 26, single, laborer; Banks, Sallie, 19, single, cook; 22 November 1870; 21 July 1871

Warner, Horace, 22, single, engineer; Reed, Annie, 21, single, servant; 20 February 1878; 26 February 1878

Warner, Levi 24, single, laborer; Watson, Emily, 26, single, servant; 27 September 1867; 14 June 1867

Warner, Perry, 33, single, farmhand; Emory, Mary C., 23, single, cook; 11 September 1885; 21 February 1885

Warren, Daniel; Ringgold, Mary A.; 28 October 1867; 18 February 1867

Warren, David, 30, widower, farmhand; Pearce, Florence, 22, single, cook; 31 March 1884; 13 June 1885

Warren, David, 36, single, laborer; Beck, Ethelin, 36, single, servant; 21 December 1868; 24 September 1869

Warrens, David E., 22, single, laborer; Thompson, Emma, 20, single, servant; 8 November 1873

Warrens, Jervis, 72, single, farmhand; Sadler, Louisa, 60, widow, cook; 3 April 1885; 20 April 1885

Washington, Cornelius, 30, single, farmhand; Warren, Emma, 21, single, servant; 20 September 1879; 16 October 1879

Washington, George; Hollins, Eliza, single, housemaid; 26 July 1870; 16 June 1870

Washington, George Thomas, 23, single, farmhand; Smith, Mary Ann, 23, single; 18 January 1878; 19 January 1872

Washington, George, 27, single, laborer; Brown, Annie, 30, widow, cook, Baltimore City; 29 November 1883; 24 June 1884

Washington, George, 28, widower, farmhand; Reed, Susan, 20, single, cook; 1 May 1884; 25 June 1884

Washington, Henry, 25, single, laborer; Wilson, R. A., 21, single, cook; 20 October 1872; 5 March 1873

Washington, Samuel, 24, single, hostler; Boyer, Willie, 19, single, cook; 5 March 1885; 20 June 1885

Washington, William L., 21, single, farmhand; Cann, Margaret, 18, single, servant; 6 December 1876; 3 February 1877

Waters, David, 31, widower, laborer; Tate, Susan A., 26, widow, servant; 1 July 1872; 5 September 1872

Waters, David, 43, widower, laborer; Chatman, Irene, 44, widow, cook; 30 December 1883; 31 March 1884

Waters, John C., 22, single, farmhand; Johnson, Maggie, 21, single, cook; 22 May 1884; 25 June 1884

Watson, John, 22, single, laborer; Smith, Caroline, 38, widow, cook; 31 October 1867; 2 February 1867

Wells, David, 22, single, farmhand; Spencer, Hannah, 17, single, cook; 14 October 1884; 24 October 1884

Wells, James H., 23, single, laborer; Cooper, Rachel, 21, single, cook; 4 June 1870; 21 July 1871

Wesley, John Wesley, 22, single, farmhand; Blake, Sarah, 20, single, cook; 10 August 1877; 21 August 1877

West, James H., 22, single, laborer; Landers (Sanders ?), Elizabeth, single, cook; 16 May 1872; 7 August 1872

Wheeler, Frederick, 23, single, farmhand; Johnson, Jane, 22, single, cook; 10 January 1885; 13 January 1885

Wheeler, Isaiah, 22, single, waiter; Miller, Ann Elizabeth, 18, single, nurse; 29 April 1883; 18 June 1883

White, Alexander, 45, widower, farmhand; Anderson, Catherine, 50, widow, servant; 4 January 1875; 8 January 1876

White, Benjamin F., 30, single, laborer; Frisby, Hannah, 28, single, cook; 14 March 1872; 7 August 1872

White, C. H., 28, single, farmhand; Whittington, Sarah, 28, single, cook; 20 November 1879; 19 January 1880

White, Daniel, 20, single, laborer; Brown, Annie, 18, single, servant; 29 November 1866; 24 April 1869

White, George Washington, 23, single, farmhand; Miller, Georgeanna, 17, single, cook; 12 April 1883; 9 May 1883

White, George, 25, single, laborer; Jones, Mary, 24, widow, cook; 20 March 1884; 13 May 1884

White, Jervis, 22, single, laborer; Lively, Elizabeth, 18, single, cook; 20 May 1880; 11 June 1880

White, Louis, 25, single, laborer; Hutchins, Sallie, single, servant; 11 October 1867; 24 April 1869

White, Sewell, 29, single, farmhand; Snowden, Ella, 28, single, cook; 27 December 1883; 13 May 1884

White, William H., 22, single, farmhand; Swigett, Catherine E., 20, single, house girl; 10 August 1882; 5 December 1882

White, William H., 32, single, laborer; Brown, Adelaide, 20, single, servant; 3 January 1867; 22 August 1867

Whittington, James, 20, single, farmhand; Wales, Wilheina, 17, single, servant; 23 September 1876; 22 October 1876

Wickes, James, single, laborer; Brooks, Lizzie, 16, servant; 5 October 1870; 3 December 1870

Wickes, Perry, 37, single, laborer; Younger, Mintie (Araminta?), 24, single, cook; 8 November 1873

Wicks, Charles, 39, single, laborer; Wallie, Amanda, 17, house servant; 24 September 1866; 14 June 1866

Wicks, Reuben, 24, single, farmhand; Rasin, Rachel, 22, widow, domestic; 22 July 1874; 31 December 1874

Wiggins, John, 27, single, farmhand; Torres, Elizabeth, 18, single; 11 October 1874; 24 July 1875

Williams, Edward, 35, single, farmhand; Johnson, Harriet, 25, single, servant; 21 May 1877; 21 July 1877

Williams, Henry, 23, single, farmhand; Thompson, Hester E., 19, single, cook; 3 October 1883; 6 October 1883

Williams, John, 20, single, farmhand; Tilghman, Mary, 21, single, cook; 13 September 1877; 22 April 1880

Williams, Mattis, 22, single, laborer; Rigby, Mary Jane, 30, single, cook; June 1870; 3 March 1871

Williams, Washington. 30, single, laborer; Gross, Maria, 15, single, servant; 14 March 1868; 8 November 1868

Willis, Charles, 23, single, laborer; Howard, Maria, 17, single, housemaid; 5 May 1870; 16 June 1870

Willson, John Henry, 23, single, laborer; Farmer, Georgia, 24, widow, servant; 18 March 1870

Wilmer, Daniel Henry, 22, single, farmhand; Wally, Emma, 20, single, servant; 6 May 1876; 13 July 1876

Wilmer, Frank, 20, single, farmhand; Woodland, Harriet, 19, single, cook; 8 January 1877; 21 August 1877

Wilmer, Henry, 21, single, farmhand; Johnson, Laura, 19, single, cook; 30 July 1885; 4 August 1885

Wilmer, Hines, 23, single, laborer; Dudley, Indiana, 21, servant; 10 December 1868; 26 July 1869

Wilmer, James H.; Rasin, Leaun Elizabeth; September 1867; 14 June 1867

Wilmer, James H., single, farmhand; Riley, Mary Lizzie, 26, single, cook; 27 December 1883; 8 February 1884

Wilmer, John W., 21, single, farmhand; Brown, Eliza L., 21, single, cook; 18 January 1879; 8 February 1879

Wilmer, Samuel J., 21, single, farmhand; Wilson, Mary C., 22, single, cook; 25 October 1883; 31 December 1883

Wilmer, Stephen, 36, widower, laborer; Wright, Amanda, single, laborer; 12 June 1879; 30 June 1873

Wilmer, Thomas, 29, single, laborer; Wilson, M. C., 26, single; 22 October 1868; 29 October 1868

Wilson, Alexander, 24, single, laborer; Ringgold, Amanda, single, cook; 20 September 1884; 15 November 1884

Wilson, Alfred, 30, single, laborer; Cane, Louisa, 28, single, service; 22 July 1867; 12 July 1869

Wilson, Alfred, 30, single, laborer; Cane, Louisa, 28, single, service; 22 July 1867; 12 July July 1869

Wilson, Alfred, 30, single, laborer; Cane, Louisa, 28, single, service; 22 July 1867; 12 July 1869

Wilson, Alfred, 30, single, laborer; Cane, Louisa, 28, single, service; 22 July 1867; 12 July 1869

Wilson, Charles Henry, 28, widower, farmer; Tiller, Isabella, 18, single, cook; 23 December 1884; 26 December 1884

Wilson, Charles, 19, single, farmer; Redding, Sarah Catherine, 19, single, servant; 17 May 1877; 12 September 1877

Wilson, Edward A., 21, single, laborer; Grooms, Nancy, 21, single, cook; 9 August 1883; 13 December 1883

Wilson, Garrett, 24, single, servant; Jones, Sarah, 21, single, servant; 9 October 1866; 4 April 1867

Wilson, George, 21, single, farmhand; Wright, Mary E., 19, single, cook; 3 December 1885; 9 January 1885

Wilson, George, 22, single, farmhand; Jones, Millie, 22 single, cook; 3 August 1882; 5 December 1882

Wilson, George, 29, single, farmhand; Benson, Ellen, 22, single, servant; 6 January 1877; 20 March 1877

Wilson, George, 29, single, farmhand; Benson, Ellen, 22, single, servant; 6 January 1877; 20 March 1877

Wilson, James, 45, widower, laborer; Demby, Matilda, 25, single, servant; 4 August 1866; 10 October 1866

Wilson, Jefferson, 26, single, laborer; Barrett, Annie, single, cook; 22 December 1868; 6 June 1869

Wilson, John H., 24, single, laborer; White, Susan, 17, single, servant; 13 October 1868; 24 September 1869

Wilson, John Henry, 22, single, farmhand; Butler, Ellen, 19, single, cook; 7 May 1882; 1 May 1883

Wilson, Joseph I., 26, single, farmhand; Brown, Emma V., 24, single, housekeeper; 3 January 1884; 5 January 1884

Wilson, Riz, 21, single, farmhand; Wilmer, Willie, 17, single, cook; 17 May 1882; 5 December 1882

Wilson, Samuel L., 26, single, farmhand; Turner, Margaret, 20, single, servant; 17 April 1879; 10 July 1879

Wing, Henry, 21, single, laborer; Kennedy, Frances S., 22, single, servant; 6 May 1870

Woodland, Emory, 44, widower, oysterman; Griffin, Ann, 35, widow, cook; 29 December 1870; 27 March 1871

Woodland, John, 24, single, laborer; Wright, Will___, 20, single, cook; 30 December 1884; 6 October 1886

Woodland, Joseph, 21, single; Wright, Isabella, 18, single, cook; 27 September 1884; 15 November 1884

Woolford, Henry, 23, single, laborer; Tillison, Mary, 18, single, servant; 13 June 1873; 12 December 1873

Wooters, Charles, 21, single, laborer; James, Sarah J., 19, single, servant; 30 May 1869; 12 July 1869

Worrell, Alfred, 26, single, laborer; Thomas, Mary E., 22, single, cook; 15 July 1884; 15 November 1884

Worrell, Asbury, 65, widower, farmhand; Freeman, Editha, 35, widow, domestic; 15 September 1876; 2 October 1876

Worrell, Richard, 21, single, farmhand; Carroll, Sallie, 18, single, cook; 15 June 1882; 1 May 1883

Wright, Daniel, 28, single, laborer; Wright, Adeline, 25, single, cook; 8 August 1872; 25 June 1873

Wright, James William, 21, single, farmhand, Queen Anne's Co; Lawrence, Q. C., 22, servant, Queen Anne's Co; 1 March 1877; 17 March 1877

Wright, Jeremiah, 25, single, farm laborer; Garrison, Henrietta, 19, single, cook; 25 September 1879; 11 November 1879

Wright, John Thomas, 23, single, farmhand; Chambers, Lydia L., 19, single, servant; 31 October 1878; 10 November 1878

Wright, John, 22, single, waiter, Queen Anne's Co; Drummond, Elizabeth, 17; 7 March 1873; 15 March 1873

Wright, Samuel, 37, single, farmhand; Emory, Hariet A., 35, single, cook; 16 December 1874; 10 April 1876

Wright, Thomas W., 21, single, laborer; Jones, Henrietta C., 18, single, servant; 15 November 1867; 14 March 1864

Wright, Thomas W., 21, single, laborer; Goldsbourough, Martha E., 27, servant; 7 October 1870; 17 February 1870; 17 October 1870

Wright, Thomas W., 35, widower, farmer; Hutchins, Carrie, 25, single, cook; 7 January 1884; 31 March 1884

Wright, Thomas, 37, single, laborer; Staten, Henrietta, 25, single, servant; 19 July 1873; 24 July 1875

Wright, William H., 25, single, farmhand; Kutler, Ellen, 18, single, servant; 24 May 1877; 12 September 1877

Wright, William, 55, widower, farmhand; Bessicks, Matilda, 45, single, cook; 21 February 1884; 26 February 1884

Wye, Willison, 38, widower, farmhand; Frisby, Maria, 34, single, cook; 27 December 1877; 23 December 1877

Yorker, Henry, 24, single, farmhand; Bowser, Charlotte, 26, single, servant; 2 February 1876; 18 February 1876

Yorker, James, 29, single, farmer; Dairy, M. E., 26, single, cook; 4 September 1879; 22 April 1880

Young, Moses, widower, laborer; Augustus, Emily, widow, servant; 1867; 14 June 1887

Brides Index

Maria 36 Marietta 42 Martha
18 Mary 12 Mary C 7 32
Mary E 13 24 Mary M 41
Mary W 11 Milly 20 Nancy
22 Priscilla 44 Rachel 34
Sarah E 27 Sarah L 24 Sarah
M 3 Willie 6
BRUNSWICK, Florence 15
BUCKNER, Mary C 18
BURDEN, Fanny 28
BURGEN, Louisa 1 Maria 23
BUTCHER, Fanny 4 Sallie 17
Sally 31 Sarah Ann 18
BUTLER, Ann E C 43 Ann
Maria 29 Annie 35 Ellen 12
52 Georgianna 21 Harriet 5
Henrietta 2 12 38 Jane 17
Lena 4 Lizzie 23 Martha 32
Mary 28 Millicent 3 Sarah 2
CAIN, M Elizabeth 46
CAMMILE, Martha A 4 Mary E
29
CAMPBELL, Alethia 19
CANE, Louisa 51
CANN, Amanda Ann 27
Margaret 49
CARROLL, Annie 19 Elizabeth
11 Hester 30 Mary 20 Nellie
18 Sallie 52 Sarah 47
CARTER, Louisa 44 Lucy 33
CASKER, Henrietta 31
CASTER, Henrietta 31
CASTLE, Marie 40
CAULK, Martha J 7 Mintie 44
CHAMBER, Lidie 19
CHAMBERS, Alice 18 Annie 13
Elizabeth 39 42 Frances M 47
Geo Anna 47 Hannah A 28
Harriet 31 Lydia L 52 Martha
37 Mary C 6 Mary E 36 Sarah
Elizabeth 9
CHAMGERS, Georgeanna 47

CHANEY, Ann Maria 9 Anna M
44 Mary 21
CHASE, Catherine 35 Louisa 36
Maria 39
CHATMAN, Irene 49 Mary
Lizzie 30
CLAYTON, Ann Maria 3
Georgianna 15
COLBERT, Annie 30
COLE, Kate 28
COLLINS, Rosanna 3 Sarah 20
COMEGYS, Ann R 33-34
Charlotte 19 Hannah 25 40
Harriet 13 Louisa 28 Mary 31
Mary R 30
COOPER, Henrietta 26 Hester 19
Jane E 19 Lizzie 32 Maria
Louisa 39 Mary L 4 Rachel
49
CORK, Ella 18
COTTON, Caroline 2 Helen 17
Julia 3 Sely Maria 14 Tempe
A 46
CRAGE, Nancy 3
CRAIG, Elizabeth 45 Nancy 3
CROSSLEY, Ann E 26
DANIELS, Cassy 33 Henrietta 24
Letis 31 Mary Francis 8
DAPSON, Eliza 44
DAVIS, Carrie 35 Charlotte 40
Ellen 9 Jane 23 Laura 41
Wilimina 33
DEAKER, Mary Ellen 41
DEMBY, Charlotte 36 Francis
Jane 18 George Ann 45
Margaret 13 Matilda 51
DENNINGS, Marianna 12
DERRY, Mary E 37
DIARY, M E 53
DICKENSON, Cora 47
DIXON, Mary E 43
DOANE, Jane 27

DOMAN, Annie 47 Harriet 21
  Lizzie 39 Mary E 14 Rosa 33
DORSEY, Eliza 46 Mary 17
  Olivia 37
DRIVER, Amy 38
DRUMMOND, Elizabeth 52
DUCKERY, Mary F 20
DUDLEY, Indiana 50
DUMAN, Mary E 14
DUNBAR, Ann Rececca 46
DUNN, Annie V 21 Lucinda 1
ELBERT, Tempy 21
ELLIOTT, Mary Eliza 14
EMORY, Charlotte 34 Hariet A
  52 Mary C 48
ENNIS, Annie 39
EVES, Martha 5
EWING, Elizabeth 39
FARMER, Georgia 50
FERRELL, Margaret 19
FINCH, Elizabeth 1
FIRSBY, Ann Rebecca 26
  Carolina 25 Sallie 28
FISHER, Georganna 7
FLAMER, Ellen 5
FLETCHER, Georgianna 24
FOGWELL, Ann E 41
FORD, Annie 41 Lillie 7
  Margaret 21 Martha A 33
FOREMAN, Caroline 28 Mary E
  38
FORMAN, Sarah E 6
FRANCIS, Mary 18
FRAZIER, Ann E 26
FREEMAN, Annie 36 Editha 12
  52 Jane 41 Julia A 26 Laura
  Jane 12 Lizzie 29 Martha 23
  Rebecca 10 17
FRISBY, Debbie 32 Hannah 49
  Julia 5 16 Lavinia 23
  Margaret 7 19 Maria 53 Mary
  9-10 Rachel 23 Salina 44 Sara
  Jane 28

GADDIS, Laura 45
GALE, ----m 15 Anna E 32
GALLISON, Martha 11
GANT, Tilly 45
GARDENER, Harriett 24
GARDNER, Hannah 8
GARNER, Harriet 8
GARRISON, Henrietta 52 Kate
  23 M Laura 40 Mary E 22
GIBBS, Emily 40 Rebecca 45
GILBERT, Melissa 20
GLEAVES, Hester Ann 33
  Louisa 28 Mary Ann 30
GLEEVES, Annie 40
GLENN, Louisa 35 Sarah C 35
GOLDSBOROUGH, Caroline 44
  Martha 38
GOLDSBOURGH, Mary Ellen
  28
GOLDSBOUROUGH, Martha E
  53
GOOLING, Jane 43
GOOSEBERRY, Martha 10
GORDON, Maria 17
GORMAN, Lizzie 24
GOSELING, Aliza 42
GOULD, Charlotte L 4 Susan 5
GRANGER, Annie 15 Hester 1
  Lizzie 21
GRAVES, Amanada 30 Anna M
  42 Elizabeth 27 Ella 34
  Georgeanna 13 Henrietta 33
  Joanna 14 Josephine 5 Lizzie
  44 Louisa 41 Margaret 46
  Maria 16 Martha 4 Mary Ann
  9 Mary E 14 Rebecca 45
  Tempy 16
GRAY, Eliza 14 Fannie 14
GREEN, Alice 22 Ella 4 Francis
  13 Jane 4 Marissa 42 Mary 47
  Matilda 26

57

GRIFFIN, Ann 52 Georgeanna
38 Harriett 34 Julia 15 Louisa
20 Sarah 30 Sarah Jane 10
GRIFFITH, Sarah 47
GRINETT, Fannie L 6
GROMMES, Elizabeth 16
GROOMS, Margaret A 31 Nancy
51
GROSS, Emma 10 Harriet C 11
Maria 50
GROVES, Milley 20
GUNN, Lucinda 1
GUSTUS, Mary 32
HACKETT, Isabella 16 Lizzie 4
Victoria 36
HALES, Louisa 37
HALL, Harriet E 18 Kitty 44
Laura 40 Louisa 14 26 Mary J
5 Mary L 40
HAMILTON, Lucinda 27 Mary
R 48
HANCE, Ella N 15
HANDY, Fanny 15 Georgianna
46 Mary Louise 11
HARDING, Alice 46
HARISTON, Anna Maria 11
HARKLESS, Sas--- 16
HARRIS, Caroline 35 Dinah 9 13
Mary Agnes 46 Mary E 16
Mary Jane 12
HARRISON, Annie 45 Editha 46
HASTINGS, Ann Rebecca 45
Ellen 36 Jane R 20
HAWKSIN, Henrietta 31
HAZEL, Arabella 45
HAZZARD, Emma 44 Mary
Drusilla 34
HEMSLEY, Delinda 1
HENRY, Sarah Maria 1
HINES, Charlotte 27
HODGES, Catherine 10 Ellen 39
HOLLINS, Eliza 48

HOPKINS, Harriet 11 Martha E
18
HORNSBY, Jane 2
HOUSTON, Ada 30 Hannah E 46
Sarah E 20
HOWARD, Maria 50
HUNSON, Mary 31
HURTT, Eliza 4
HUSTON, Rachael 13
HUTCHINS, Carrie 53 Margaret
30 Sallie 50 Teresa 19
HYLAND, Delia 32
HYNSON, Annie E 35 Augusta E
11 Caroline 39 Ella 37 Ellen
39 Francis 22 Geo Anna 47
Harriet A 4 Letitia 13 Lizzie
26 Louisa 16 Martha 29 Mary
Jane 25 Sarah C 9
IRVING, Mary Francis 39
JACKSON, Teena 32 Tiny 1
JACOBS, Annie 2
JAMES, H A 9 Jane 17 Sarah J
52
JEFFERS, Augusta 36
JENKINS, Alice 19 Elizabeth 13
Gracy A 35
JOHNS, Annie 40
JOHNSON, Adeline 39 Anna 11
Annie M 47 Carrie 43 Charlot
A 34 Charlotte 33-34 Clara 24
Eliza 28 Elizabeth 17 45
Emma 27 Emma J 8 Fannie
33 Harriet 50 Harriet E 45
Hattie A 10 Henrietta 32
Hester 36 Jane 49 Jane H 25
Laura 41 50 Lotty Ann 27
Lucy Ann 26 Maggie 49
Margaret 18 Maria 3 17 Mary
25 Mary A 6 Mary D 23
Matilda 21 Milcah 36 Susan
Ann 30
JONES, A M A 3 Alice J 45
Annie 19 Augusta 1 Dollie 11

Eliza A 42 Elizabeth 5-6 Ella
14 Ellen 35 48 Georganna 43
Hannah Liz 10 Harriet 38
Harriett Rebecca 4-5
Henrietta C 52 Hester 1 Jane
41 Linda 37 Lizzie 21 Marion
15 Mary 8 49 Mary A 1 Mary
C 30 Mary E 22 Mary J 9
Millie 51 Minty 11 Rachel 37
Sarah 29 51 Sarah Elizabeth
25 Sarah Lizzie 35
KELLUM, Rosie 21
KELLY, Sarah G 42
KENNARD, Araminta 28
Elizabeth 17 Harriet 18 Jane 2
23 Jennie E 15 Margaret 12
Martha 38
KENNEDY, Frances S 52
KEVER, Emery 8
KEYS, Lizzie 2
KILSON, H E M 47
KIRBY, Annie E 47
KUTLER, Ellen 53
LAMDEN, Susie Clara 41
LANDERS, Elizabeth 49
LAWRENCE, Elizabeth 33 Q C
52
LAWS, Mollie 33
LEATHERBERRY, Caroline 7
30
LEE, Georgianna 34 Prissy 7
Sarah M 37
LEIAS, Alice 48
LINDSEY, Chloe A 22 Mary 39
LIVELY, Adeline 48 Anna Maria
17 Catherine 10 Elizabeth 49
Mary 10 Nancy 27
LYLE, Sallie 21
MACCON, Susan 9
MADDON, Charlotte 23
MADISON, Frances 3
MANDER, Mary Ellen 15 Sallie
24 Sally 17

MASON, Alberta 40 Mary Ann
30 Mary J 32
MASSEY, Lydia 21 Mary 18 24
MATHIAS, Eliza 2
MATINEY, Mary 8
MATTHEWS, Ophelia 15
MCGRAITH, Amanda 47
MEEDS, Martha 20
MERCHANT, Alice 24
MERIDTH, Henrietta 15
MILES, Hester Ann 11
MILLER, Ann Elizabeth 49 Ann
M 36 Ann Maria 8
Georgeanna 49 Louisa 9
Martha Jane 43 Mary Ellen 25
Mary Louisa 18 Octavia 42
Rachel 37 Sallie 17 Sarah
Maria 42
MILLIGAN, Hester Ann 31
MITCHELL, Alverta 19 Annie
10 Lena 13 Lucy 27
MONTGOMERY, Eleanor 17
MOODY, Mary E 30
MOORE, Ella 3 Harriet 30 Julia
A 23 Mary I 45
MORGAN, Hattie 15 Jennie 48
MORLOCK, Annie 14
MOROCCO, Lydia A 13
MUNSON, Bell J 10 Belle J 10
Georgianna 12 Henrietta 22
MURRAY, Catherine 15 29
Harriet 28 Jane 24 Lydia 5
Maria 15 Martha 19 Mary 41
MURREY, Sarah Ann 45
MYERS, Annie 38
NEAL, Louisa 1
NEWMAN, Anna M 3
NICHOLS, Ella 28 Rachel I 22
NIHCOLS, Ann 6
OAKLEY, Mary Ann 12
PALMER, Clara 27
PEAKER, Lon 10

59

PEARCE, Elizabeth 12 Florence
48 Jane 34 Laura 44
PENNICK, Emily 21
PERKINS, Anna M 16 Fanny 28
PERRY, Rebecca 37
PHILIPS, Nancy J 23
PHILLETT, Annie Amelia 26
PHILLIPS, Hester A 35 Jane 31
Laura 30
PHIMONER, Kitty 28
PIERCE, Harret 34
PINER, Becky 35
PLATER, Lizzie 1 Louisa 14
POICE, Hannah E 25
PORTER, Henrietta 45
POSEY, Eliza 29
POSTMAN, Sarah L 24
PRICE, Caroline 37 Mary 18
PURPOSE, Susan 30
RAISIN, Julia 24 Rachel S 1
Victoria 29
RASIN, Ann 14 Annie 13 Laura
37 Leaun Elizabeth 51
Margaret 32 Mary E 8 12
Rachel 50 Sallie 31 Sarah M
46 Victoria 23
RASISN, Jane Louisa 39
REASON, Ella 8
REDDING, Ann E 43 Annie 34
Fannie 10 Martha 26 Mary
Elizabeth 9
REED, Amanda Jane 31 Annie
48 Augusta 27 Debby 38
Emma 41 Mary 25 Sarah 21
Susan 49
REES, Annie Ell 6
REESE, Elizabeth 15 Emma 1
REYNOLDS, Henrietta 4
RICHARDS, Eliza D 24
RICKETT, Sarah 25
RIELY, Susan 34
RIGBY, Elizabeth 36 Mary Jane
50

RILEY, Araminta 32 Catherine
31 Eliza 43 Harriet A 6
Martha D 42 Martha J 25
Mary Lizzie 51 Mary M 27
RINGGOLD, Amanda 25 51
Annie 24 Augustus 46
Hannah 3 Hannah E 3
Henrietta 4 Laura 22 Mary A
48 Minty 7 Rachel 44 Rachel
A 28 Sarah 35 Temperence C
27
ROBERTS, Araminta 32 Mintie
17
ROBINSON, Margaret 34
ROE, Julia 36
ROGERS, Polly Ann 20
ROLETERS, Sarah R 12
RONER, Mary E 8
ROSS, Sarah E 46
ROULETTE, Temperence 12
RUSSELL, Mary E 24
SADLER, Louisa 48
SAGES, Henrietta 29
SALTER, Caroline 48
SANDERS, Anna R 6 Betsy 29
Elizabeth 49 Helen 35
Henrietta 13 Jane L 18 Rachel
25
SARAH, Catherine 51
SAUNDERS, Florence 21
Henrietta 13 Jane 36 Julia 7
SCOTT, Addie 41 Adeline 19
Annie 10 Betsy 19 Carolyn 25
Elizabeth 38 Hester 6 Lucy 22
Mary L 32 Matilda 24 Sarah 1
47
SEENEY, Henrietta 8 Julia 32
SEGAR, Jane 47
SEGG, Mary 46
SENEY, Irene 40 Lydia 16
Martha Jane 40
SHEPPARD, Annie 37 Editha 21

SHIELDS, Annie M 41 Rachel
   33
SIMMONS, Ellen 3
SINGLE, Annie 39
SMALLWOOD, Clara 36 Martha
   43
SMITH, Anna 15 Caroline 49
   Deborah A 20 Gracie 5
   Henrietta 27 Isabel 43 Mary
   A 40 Mary Ann 48 Susan 9
   Welthy 22
SNOWDEN, Eliza 42 Ella 50
SPENCER, Annie J 36 Araminta
   33 Elizabeth 44 Emeline 30
   Emily L 21 Hannah 49 Julia
   A 33 Lucy 4 M A 25 Mary E
   25
STANLEY, Hester Ann 9
STARLING, Anna L 16 Annie 43
   Caroline 7 Florence 16 Mary
   32 Mary A 29 Mary Louise
   16
STATEN, Henrietta 53
STEVENS, Mamie 12
STEWARD, Lizzie 3
STEWART, Agnes 35 Angelina
   28 Catherine 40 Harriett 33
   Mary E 20 Susan 18
SUDLER, Julia 5
SWIETT, Catherine E 50
TANNER, Amanda 25 Annie 9
TATE, Susan A 49
TEMPY, Ann Veal 6
THOMAS, Alethia 9 Amanda 37
   Ann Rebecca 42 Anna 43
   Annie 10 Augusta 32 Eliza 28
   Elizabeth Jane 8 Ella 43 Irene
   14 Julia 24 Lizzie 6 Louisa 44
   Margaret 20 Martha J 43
   Mary C 45 Mary E 11 52
   Mary Jane 13 Rachel 41
   Sarah 19 Sophie 29

THOMPSON, Alice 4 Ann
   Rebecca 26 Caroline 35
   Elizabeth 44 Ellen 2 Emma
   48 Frances A 9 Gingr 42
   Henrietta 2 32 Hester E 50
   Louisa 12 Martha I 20 Mary
   27 Mary J 39 Mary L 19
   Mary R 9 Rachel 42
THOMSON, Sarah E 18
TILGHMAN, Alphonsa 37 Annie
   3 Caroline 21 38 Edith 46
   Emily Elizabeth 47 Henrietta
   37 Julia J 36 Mary 29 50
   Rachel 35 Rosetta 15 Susan
   42
TILLER, Isabella 51
TILLERSON, Mary E 26
TILLISON, Annie 40 Mary 1 52
TOOMY, Catherine 42 Easter J 2
TORRES, Elizabeth 50
TOULSON, Harriet Ann 44
TOWSON, Lizzie Ann 17
TRUSTY, 11 Anna M 22 Hannah
   1 Henrietta 39 Jane 11
TUNER, L I 45
TURNER, Emma 1 Georgianna 5
   Lizzie 22 Margaret 52 Martha
   25 Mary Isabella 4 Nancy 33
URIE, Emeline 38
VICKERSON, Violena 13
WAILES, Robertine 21
WALKER, Annie R 43 Mary 24
WALLEY, Catherine 16 Luoisa
   33
WALLIE, Amanda 50
WALLIS, Anna 27 Lizzie 17
   Mary Jane 35 Rachel 7
WALLY, Emma 50
WARD, Anna 41 Augustus 42
   Catherine 23 Julia 1 Sarah 13
   Susan Jane 38
WARNER, Anna Maria 37
   Henrietta 8 Katie 44

WARREN, Emma 48
WASHINGTON, Fannie J 26
   Florence 31
WASLES, Wilheina 50
WATERS, Mary E 29
WATSON, Ella 18 Emily 48
WELCH, Louisa 29
WELLS, Amanda 34 Louisa 16
WHALE, Mary 30
WHEEDERS, Sadie 30
WHEELER, Sadie 30
WHITE, Araminta 27 Catherine
   47 Clarissa Ann 17 Edie E 20
   Hariet M 41 Laura 27 Maria
   40 Mary A 36 Rosa C B 10
   Susan 52
WHITTINGHAM, Nancy 2
WHITTINGTON, Emeline 12
   Sarah 49
WICKER, Mary Matilda 26
WICKES, Mary J 37 Sallie 45
WICKS, Mary L 31
WIGGINS, Susan 17
WILLIAMS, Eliza 44 Lizzie 25
   Nancy 23
WILLIS, Ann 41
WILLSON, Mary 46
WILMER, Alice A 6 Annie 16
   Dorothia 31 Ella Jane 2
   Georgetta 33 Laura L 40
   Mary E 12 Mary Jand 45
   Willie 52

WILMOR, Laura J 43
WILSON, Ann M 31 Annie F 19
   Clara 31 Editha 5 13
   Elizabeth 20 Ellen 46 Emma
   34 Frances 8 Harriet 38
   Harriet Ann 23 Isabella 18
   Kate 14 Lizzie 17 26 M C 51
   Margaret 25 Martha 45 Mary
   C 51 Mary J 31 R A 49 Rosa
   35 Susan 38 43
WING, Anna Maria 40
WOODLAND, Annie 11 Harriet
   50 Jane 41 Jessie 31 Julia 46
   Mary 27
WOODS, Harriet 30
WOOLFORD, Elizabeth 16
WORRELL, Charlotte 43 Hester
   V 35 Mary Ann 24 Susan 4
WRIGHT, Adeline 52 Amanda
   51 Eliza 26 48 Ella 42 Emily
   6 26 Emma A 1 Fanny 27
   Henrietta 29 42 Isabella 52
   Lizzie 6 Mary E 51 Mary
   Ellen 24 Mary F 7 Rachel 20
   Will____ 52
YORKER, Louise 20 Mary
   Elizabeth 19
YOUNG, Amanda 37 Martha A
   11
YOUNGER, Araminta 50 Mintie
   50
_ALTER, Mary C 32